KB264404

EVERY MAN'S
Korean Conversation

PREFACE

Korea is a fascinating country from the standpoint of culture, history, and geography and so forth. Touring and conducting business in this country, as in other parts of the world, require communication adequate enough to enhance your appreciation of beauty both cultural and natural, to generate the interest of your customer in your products, and thus to create and/or expand your markets. Whether your purpose of visiting Korea is sightseeing or strict business or diplomacy, this handbook will provide you with the most useful phrases and expressions to suit your need to communicate efficiently and confidently.

With a special phonetic key, this book will give you

(1) an easy-to-follow pronunciation guide,

(2) a complete phonetic transcription for every word and phrase introduced,

(3) a handy glossary of basic terms and expressions characteristic of the Korean language

(4) a list of common abbreviations pertaining to business, and

(5) practical words and phrases covering a wide range of everyday topics and situations.

The publication of this handbook was made possible by support from the president of Samji Publishing Company. We express our sincerest appreciation for the kind encouragement he rendered while we were preparing the manuscript.

CONTENTS

INTRODUCTION

1. Alphabet and Pronunciation

(1) Alphabet

The Korean writing system is called hangul which is a kind of method of representing the sounds of phonemes. Contrary to what you've probably heard, the Korean language is not difficult to speak. In fact, some people believe it's simpler than other languages because it lacks some linguistic 'headaches'(such as inflections, declensions, conjugations, genders, or verb tenses or moods). Just think of English verbs for a moment and you'll see what we mean. So-called regular verbs(like 'talk' or 'offer') have four different forms in English, and the irregular verbs(like 'do', 'give' or 'see') have at least five possible forms. Any verb in English has five properties(person, number, tense, voice, and mood), and any one of them affects the verb making it different in form under different circumstances. The Korean language has none of these problems. Korean grammar consists primarily of rules for word order rather than rules for word change. Basically, the Korean alphabet consists of 14 consonants(C's) and 10 vowels(V's) which, when put together in the order of CV or CVC or CVCC, form syllables which in turn constitute vocabulary words. In this book, we have adopted Revised system of transcription to show the utterances of Hangul in romanized letters.

Experience with another foreign language will be useful in uttering as well aw responding to the Korean language. But don't worry if you haven't had such experience. This book with its several aids will be of great help to you. Remember that a little effort to make use of the language goes a long way in a foreign country. The Korean you meet will be delighted that you have tried to learn their language, and will be quite willing to help you for your needs.

Koreans are justly proud of much in their culture. And among their many achievements, they are perhaps most proud of their unique language, with its unbroken tradition spanning thousands of years.

(2) Pronunciation

The basic sounds of the Korean language are not hard to hear or to reproduce with practice. There are only a few sounds such as [v] and [f] in the Korean language those do not occur in English.

CONSONANTS

HANGEUL NOTATION	ROMANI-ZATION	KOREAN(ENGLISH) NOTATION
ㄱ	k, g	고구마 *goguma*(sweet potato)
ㄴ	n	나 *na* (I)
ㄷ	t, d	다리미 *darimi* (iron)
ㄹ	r, l	라면 *ramyeon* (noodle)

ㅁ	m	모자 *moja* (hat)
ㅂ	p, b	바지 *ba-ji* (pants)
ㅅ	s, sh	사람 *saram* (man)
ㅇ	silent letter*	아버지 *abeoji* (father)
ㅇ	ng	병 *byeong* (bottle)
ㅈ	ch, j	자동차 *jadongcha* (car)
ㅊ	ch	차례 *charye* (order)
ㅋ	k	카메라 *kamera* (camera)
ㅌ	t	타조 *tajo* (a bird)
ㅍ	p	파마 *pama* (perm.)
ㅎ	h	하늘 *haneul* (sky)

*when used as initial sound

In addition, there are 5 compound consonants in the Korean alphabet.

ㄲ	kk	stressed sound of 「ㄱ」 까만색 *kkaman-saek* (black)
ㄸ	tt	stressed sound of 「ㄷ」 떡 *tteok* (rice bread)
ㅃ	pp	stressed sound of 「ㅂ」 빵 *ppang* (bread)
ㅆ	ss	stressed sound of 「ㅅ」 쌀 *ssal* (rice)
ㅉ	jj	stressed sound of 「ㅈ」 찜질방 *jjimjilbang* (sauna)

Besides basic 11 consonants and 5 compound consonants, there are 10 basic vowels.

VOWELS

HANGEUL NOTATION	ROMANI- ZATION	KOREAN(ENGLISH) NOTATION
아	a	아기 *a–gi* (child)
야	ya	야구공 *ya–gu–gong* (baseball)
어	eo	어머니 *eomeo–ni* (mother)
여	yeo	여름 *yeoreum* (summer)
오	o	오리 *o–ri* (duck)
요	yo	요구 *yogu* (demand)
우	u	우리 *uri* (we)
유	yu	유리창 *yurichang* (window)
으	eu	으뜸 *eu–tteum* (first)
이	i	이발 *i–bal* (haircut)
요	yo	요리 *yo–ri* (food)

There are 11 compound vowels as following.

애	ai or ae sound as in	'a' man
얘	yai or yae sound as in	'ya' yam
에	e sound as in	'e' egg
예	ye sound as in	'ye' yellow
외	oi or oe sound as in	'we' wet
위	ui or wi sound as in	'wee' weed
의	ui sound as in	'uoy' in buoy
와	oa or wa sound as in	'wa' swallow
워	ueo or wo sound as in	'wo' wonderful
왜	oai or wae sound as in	'wa' wax
웨	ue or we sound as in	'we' well

2. Syllables

A syllable is a sound or a short sequence of sounds which contains one peak of sonority. The peak is usually a vowel, which is the nucleus of syllable. An utterance contains as many syllables as there are peaks. In the Korean language, each sound makes a syllable. Examples are as the following :

   1) Consonant + vowel

     ㄴ + ㅏ → 나[*na*] I

   2) Consonant + vowel + consonant

     ㅇ + ㅕ + ㄴ → 연[*yeon*] kite

Phonetic assimilation is very common in the Korean language as it is in English. For instance, the actual spelling of the word 'apnal' meaning 'future' is 앞날. But it is pronounced as 암날(amnal) because the consonant 'ㅍ' sounds like 'ㅁ' when it proceeds a nasal consonant such as 'ㄴ'. When writing the 'hanguk' we find another phonetic change occurs between syllables where the final sound 'ㄴ'(n) of the syllable is preceded by 'ㄱ'(g) of the next syllable. In some other cases, phonemic changes occur between symbols. That is, the actual pronunciation differs from the written letter.

1) We often use the hyphen (-) in order to set off the stem from its affix or in order to demarcate the boundary of pronunciation clearly. That is, they are used, when necessary, to distinguish a sound between syllables, to help lengthen a sound, and to separate grammatical functions.

토요일	*to-yo-il* (Saturday)
한국	*han-guk* (another name of Korea)
아침	*a-chim* (morning)
사람	*sa-ram* (man)
정구	*jeong-gu* (tennis)
남자	*nam-ja* (male)

2) The romanization of hangul is based on the actual sound.

e.g.

신 + 라	*shin + ra → shilla*
앞 + 날	*ap - nal → amnal*
식 + 량	*shik + ryang → shingnyang*

3) Depending on the environment, sounds such as ㄱ (k, g), ㄷ (t, d), ㅂ (p, b), ㅈ (ch, j) can result in voiced sound or voiceless sound in the phrase or word. Sounds

like these are romanized with two different symbols. In the initial position they are accompanied by aspiration. Thus we distinguish between 'g' and 'k', 't' and 'd', 'p' and 'b' and 'ch' and 'j'. But now sounds of these are romanized only with 'g', 'd', 'b', 'j'.

e.g.

① 거리　　　*geo-ri* (street) 〉 *keo-ri*
　도구　　　*do-gu* (tool)
② 다리미　　*da-ri-mi* (iron) 〉 *ta-ri-mi*
　군대　　　*gun-dae* (troop) 〉 *kun-dae*
③ 전화　　　*jeon-hwa* (phone) 〉 *cheon-hwa*
　자전거　　*ja-jeon-geo* (bicycle)
　　　　　　〉 *cha-jeon-geo*
④ 보리　　　*bo-ri* (barley) 〉 *po-ri*
　이불　　　*i-bul* (sheet)

PART I
BASIC WORDS AND PHRASES

1. What you need for your flight

Don't arrive at the airport at the last minute. Every time you fly be sure to get there an hour before your flight. If you want someone to meet you at your destination, let him know the details of your flight : your carrier, flight number, time of arrival, and the name of the Korean airport you are arriving at. Otherwise, something you've never expected may happen. He can be waiting at one airline terminal when you have arrived at another, quite a distance apart.

All foreigners must have passports. You can apply for it by mail or in person in your country. Consult your travel agency or international airline office. They will inform you about what documents you need to prepare and the proper procedures to follow. No international airline offices can issue international travel tickets without valid passports.

Visas are not required for travel to Korea with confirmed outbound tickets for a stay that does not exceed 15 days. Korean embassy or consulates issues two kinds of visa : short-term visa and long term visa.

① Those who are supposed to stay for less than 90 days need only a short-term visa.

② Those who choose to stay more than 90 days need to have a long-term visa as well as an entry permit from the Ministry of Justice.

Most hotels, restaurants, and reputable shops accept major international traveler's checks and credit cards such as Master's Card, Diners Club, American Express, and VISA, etc. Remember that the exchange rate on traveler's checks may be somewhat disadvantageous to you.

The expressions in this section are those you'll use again and again - they are the fundamental building blocks of conversation. They will be of great help to you when expressing your wants or needs. Besides they include some simple question forms. We suggest that you familiarize yourself with the following phrases.

Listed below are many short phrases that will be useful in many of the social situations already presented. Try to learn as many as you can and use them often as your situation requires.

Excuse me.

_ 실례합니다. (to get attention)
sillyehamnida.

_ 미안합니다. (to apologize)
mianhamnida.

Welcome!

환영합니다.
hwanyeonghamnida.

I'm very sorry.

매우 죄송합니다.
mae-u joesonghamnida.

Thank you (very much).

매우 감사합니다.
mae-u gamsahamnida.

May I trouble you?

수고 좀 해 주시겠습니까?

sugo jom hae jusigetseumnikka?

Good.

좋습니다.

joseumnida.

Very good.

매우 좋습니다.

mae-u joseumnida.

Wonderful.

너무나 좋습니다.

neomuna joseumnida.

You are welcome.

천만에요.

cheonmaneyo.

Don't hurry.

서두르지 마세요.

seodureuji maseyo.

No problem.

문제없습니다.

munje eopseumnida.

Yes.

예 or 네

ye or ne

Right.

맞습니다.

matseumnida.

No.

아닙니다.

animnida.

Sir.

선생님

seonsaengnim

Excuse me.

실례합니다.

sillyehamnida.

Hello(by phone)

여보세요.

yeoboseyo.

Please.

어서/좀

eoseo/jom

Please say it again.

다시 말씀 좀 해주세요.

dasi malsseum jom haejuseyo.

Mr.

선생님

seonsaengnim

Miss

양

yang

Mrs.

여사

yeosa

Of course.

> 물론입니다.

> *mullonimnida.*

O.K./Fine./All right.

> 좋습니다.

> *joseumnida.*

Maybe(possibility).

> 그럴 겁니다.

> *geureol geomnida.*

No thanks.

> 괜찮습니다.

> *gwaenchanseumnida.*

It's all right.

> 상관없습니다.

> *sanggwan-eopseumnida.*

It doesn't matter.

> 문제없습니다.

> *munje-eopseumnida.*

Oh, I see.

아, 그렇군요.

a, geureokunyo.

Is that so?

그래요?

geuraeyo?

Really?(Is it true?)

정말예요?

jeongmaryeyo?

I think so.

그렇게 생각합니다.

geureoke saenggakamnida.

I don't think so.

그렇게 생각하지 않습니다.

geureoke saenggakaji anseumnida.

Wait a minute.

잠깐만요.

jamkkanmanyo.

Yes, it is.

네, 그렇습니다.

ne, geureoseumnida.

Right away.

즉시.

jeuksi.

Don't mention it.

별말씀을 다 하십니다.

byeolmalsseumeul da hasimnida.

See you later.

나중에 또 봅시다.

najung-e tto bopsida.

How are things with you?

어떻게 지내십니까?

eotteoke jinaesimnikka?

Pardon me.

실례합니다.

sillyehamnida.

Have a good trip.

좋은 여행이 되시기를 바랍니다.

joeun yeohaeng-i doesigireul baramnida.

Have a good time.

즐거운 시간 되시기 바랍니다.

jeulgeoun sigan doesigi baramnida.

That's fine.

좋습니다.

joseumnida.

It doesn't matter.

문제될 것 없습니다.

munjedoel geot eopseumnida.

That's the truth!

맞습니다.

matseumnida.

Here is my card.

제 명함입니다.

je myeonghamimnida.

Wait a moment.

잠깐만요.

jamkkanmanyo.

I think so.

저도 그렇게 생각합니다.

Jeodo geureoke saenggakamnida.

I don't think so.

저는 그렇게 생각하지 않습니다.

jeoneun geureoke saenggakaji anseumnida.

You are right.

맞습니다.

matseumnida.

I'm wrong.

제가 틀렸습니다.

jega teullyeotseumnida.

Happy birthday!

기쁜 생일을 맞이하시기를!

gippeun saeng-ireul majihasigireul!

Please come in.

듣어오세요.

deureo-oseyo.

Please sit down.

앉으세요.

anjeuseyo.

Good luck.

행운을 빕니다.

haeng-uneul bimnida.

When	Where
언제	어디서
eonje	*eodiseo*
Who	What
누가	무엇을
nuga	*mu-eoseul*

Why

왜

wae

How

어떻게

eotteoke

What's this?

이것은 무엇입니까?

igeoseun mu-eosimnikka?

How much is this?

이것은 얼마입니까?

igeoseun eolmaimnikka?

What's the matter with you?

왜 그러십니까?

wae geureosimnikka?

Where's the station?

정거장이 어디에 있습니까?

jeong-geojang-i eodie itseumnikka?

How long have you been in Korea?

한국에 얼마나 있었습니까?

han-guge eolmana isseotseumnikka?

I would like to <u>marriage</u>.

> 결혼하고 싶습니다.
>
> *gyeolhon hago sipseumnida.*

I would like to eat <u>potatoes</u>.

> 감자을/를 먹고 싶습니다.
>
> *gamja eul/reul meokgo sipseumnida.*

I want to <u>concellation</u>.

> 취소하고 싶습니다.
>
> *chwiso hago sipseumnida.*

Could you give me <u>chicken</u>?

> 닭고기을/를 주시겠습니까?
>
> *dakgogi eul/reul jusigetseumnikka?*

I want to drink a cup of water

> 물을 마시고 싶습니다.
>
> *mureul masigo sipseumnida.*

I want to buy <u>purse</u>.

지갑을/를 사고 싶습니다.

jigap eul/reul sago sipseumnida.

I need <u>solt</u>.

소금이/가 필요합니다.

sogeum i/ga piryohamnida.

Would you show me the way to <u>lake</u>?

호수로 가는 길을 알려 주시겠습니까?

hosu ro ganeun gireul allyeo jusi-getseumnikka?

Thank you very much.

대단히 감사합니다.

daedanhi gamsahamnida.

(4) Forms of Address

Listed below are traditional forms of address, which are extensively used.

Sir Kim	Madam Lee
김 선생님	이 여사님
Kim seonsaengnim	*i yeosanim*
Mrs. Go	**Miss Hong**
미세스 고	홍 양
miseseu go	*hong yang*

Mr. Jang

장 씨

jang ssi

(5) Personal Conditions

I'm thirsty.

저 목마른데요.

jeo mongmareundeyo.

I'm sick.

저 아픈데요.

jeo apeundeyo.

I'm hungry.

저 배고픈데요.

jeo baegopeundeyo.

I'm full.

저 배부릅니다.

jeo baebureumnida.

I'm tired.

저 피곤한데요.

jeo pigonhandeyo.

I'm all right.

저는 괜찮습니다.

jeoneun gwaenchanseumnida.

I'm sleepy.

저는 졸린데요.

jeoneun jollindeyo.

Please give me a bill.

청구서 좀 주세요.

cheongguseo jom juseyo.

Let's make an appointment.

약속을 합시다.

yaksogeul hapsida.

Let me know your address.

주소 좀 알려주세요.

juso jom allyeojuseyo.

Can I rent a car?

차를 빌릴 수 있습니까?

chareul billil su itseumnikka?

Do you have a check?

수표를 가지고 있습니까?

supyoreul gajigo itseumnikka?

What's the date today?

오늘은 며칠입니까?

oneureun myeochirimnikka?

Do you want the documents?

서류를 원하십니까?

seoryureul wonhasimnikka?

Where is the elevator?

승강기가 어디에 있습니까?

seungganggiga eodie itseumnikka?

This is my friend.

이 사람은 제 친구입니다.

i sarameun je chin-gu-imnida.

Please give me a hanger.

옷걸이 좀 주세요.

otgeori jom juseyo.

Here is your key.

여기 당신의 열쇠가 있습니다.

yeogi dangsinui yeolsoega itseumnida.

Would you like to make a list?

목록을 만드시겠습니까?

mongnogeul mandeusigetseumnikka?

How much is this magazine?

이 잡지는 얼마입니까?

i japjineun eolma-imnikka?

Are you the manager?

당신이 지배인입니까?

dangsini jibaeinimnikka?

Where is the map?

지도가 어디에 있습니까?

jidoga eodie itseumnikka?

Don't make a mistake.

실수하지 마십시오.

silsuhaji masipsio.

Do you have some money?

돈 좀 가지고 있습니까?

don jom gajigo itseumnikka?

What is your name?

이름이 무엇입니까?

ireumi mu−eosimnikka?

Here is today's newspaper.

오늘 신문이 여기 있습니다.

oneul sinmuni yeogi itseumnida.

Is this your office?

여기가 당신의 사무실입니까?

yeogiga dangsinui samusirimnikka?

Please help me bring my package.

내 소포 가져오는 것 좀 도와주세요.

nae sopo gajeooneun geot jom dowajuseyo.

Do you have some tissues?

휴지가 있습니까?

hyujiga itseumnikka?

We need raincoats.

비옷이 필요합니다.

biosi piryohamnida.

I would like to make a reservation.

예약을 하고 싶습니다.

yeyageul hago sipseumnida.

Where is a Western restaurant?

양식집이 어디에 있습니까?

yangsikjibi eodie itseumnikka?

Can I buy shirts here?

여기서 셔츠를 살 수 있습니까?

yeogiseo syeocheureul sal su itseumnikka?

(7) Useful Antonyms

above/below

위에/아래에

wie/arae-e

ahead/behind

먼저/뒤에

meonjeo/dwie

beautiful/ugly

아름다운/미운

areumdaun/miun

big/small

큰/작은

keun/jageun

best

가장 좋은

gajang joeun

worst

가장 나쁜

gajang nappeun

dark/light

어두운/밝은

eoduun/balgeun

delicious/bitter

달콤한/쓴

dalkomhan/sseun

early/late

일찍/늦게

iljjik/neutge

easy/difficult

쉬운/어려운

swiun/eoryeoun

expensive/cheap

값비싼/값싼

gapbissan/gapssan

few/many

적은/많은

jeogeun/maneun

first/ last

처음/마지막

cheo-eum/majimak

front/back

앞/뒤

ap/dwi

full/empty

가득 찬/빈

gadeuk chan/bin

good/bad

좋은/나쁜

jo-eun/nappeun

heavy

무거운

mugeoun

light

가벼운

gabyeoun

hot

더운

deoun

cold

차가운

chagaun

intelligent

총명한

chongmyeonghan

stupid

어리석은

eoriseogeun

inside/outside

안에/밖에

ane/bakke

large/small

큰/작은

keun/jageun

more

더 많은

deo maneun

less

더 적은

deo jeogeun

near/far

가까운/먼

gakkaun/meon

old/new

오랜/새로운

oraen/saeroun

strong	weak
튼튼한	약한
teunteunhan	*yakan*
quiet	noisy
조용한	시끄러운
joyonghan	*sikkeureoun*
warm	cool
따스한	시원한
ttaseuhan	*siwonhan*
same	different
똑같은	다른
ttokgateun	*dareun*
young	old
나이어린	나이든
na-ieorin	*na-ideun*
open	shut
열려있는	닫힌
yeollyeo-inneun	*dachin*

right/wrong	slow/fast
옳은/그른	느린/빠른
oreun/geureun	*neurin/ppareun*
thin	thick
엷은	두꺼운
yeolbeun	*dukkeoun*
wide	narrow
폭이 넓은	폭이 좁은
pogi neolbeun	*pogi jobeun*

(8) Directions

north/south	east/west
북/남	동/서
buk/nam	*dong/seo*
at the corner	straight ahead
구석에서	곧장, 똑바로
guseogeseo	*gotjang, ttokbaro*

left

왼쪽

oenjjok

right

오른쪽

oreunjjok

middle

가운데

gaunde

What day is it today?

오늘이 무슨 요일입니까?

oneuri museun yoirimnikka?

It's <u>Tuesday</u>.

<u>화</u>요일입니다.

<u>*hwa*</u> *yoirimnida.*

Sunday

일요일

iryoil

Monday

월요일

woryoil

Tuesday	Wednesday
화요일	수요일
hwayoil	*suyoil*
Thursday	Friday
목요일	금요일
mogyoil	*geumyoil*
Saturday	yesterday
토요일	어제
toyoil	*eoje*
today	the day before yesterday
오늘	그저께
oneul	*geujeokke*
tomorrow	the day after tomorrow
내일	모레
nae-il	*more*
week	this week
주	금주
ju	*geumju*

last week

지난주

jinanju

next week

다음 주

daeum ju

for one week

일주일 동안

iljuil dong-an

for two weeks

이주일 동안

ijuil dong-an

in one week

일주일 만에

iljuil mane

in the afternoon

오후에

ohu-e

in the early evening

초저녁에

chojeonyeoge

in the evening

저녁에

jeonyeoge

in one day

하루 만에

haru mane

in two days

이틀 만에

iteul mane

three days ago

사흘 전

saheul jeon

this morning

오늘 아침

oneul achim

this afternoon

오늘 오후

oneul ohu

tonight

오늘 밤

oneul bam

tomorrow night

내일 밤

naeil bam

in the morning

아침에

achime

by morning

아침까지

achimkkaji

by Tuesday

화요일까지

hwayoilkkaji

weekday

주중

jujung

weekend

주말

jumal

everyday

매일

maeil

work day

근무일

geunmuil

per day

하루에

haru-e

during the week

주중에

jujung-e

a week from today on

오늘부터 일주일 간

oneulbuteo iljuil gan

spring

봄

bom

summer

여름

yeoreum

autumn

가을

ga-eul

winter

겨울

gyeo-ul

2. Phrases for Survival

You may not speak a word of Korean but, if you memorize the next set of phrases, you will be able to impress people as a person of good manners and start accumulating basic knowledge of things you encounter in a new setting. Remember that 'insa' or saying 'hi' is regarded as a very nice and important gesture when you meet someone for the first time and any time you see her or him again.

(1) Useful Expressions

I am pleased to meet you (lit. "I see you for the first time"). Let me introduce myself.

My name is <u>John</u>.

저는 존입니다.

jeoneun jon imnida.

Excuse me.

실례합니다.

sillyehamnida.

Thank you.

고맙습니다.

gomapseumnida.

See you again.

다시 뵙겠습니다.

dasi boepgetseumnida.

Hello.

여보세요.

yeoboseyo.

Please help me.

좀 도와주십시오.

jom dowajusipsio.

What's that?

저것은 무엇입니까?

jeogeoseun mu-eosimnikka?

What's this?

이것은 무엇입니까?

igeoseun mu-eosimnikka?

How do I get to <u>information</u>?

<u>안내소</u>는/은 어떻게 갑니까?

<u>annaeso</u> neun/eun eotteoke gamnikka?

Where is <u>exit</u>?

<u>출구</u>는/은 어디에 있습니까?

<u>chulgu</u> neun/eun eodie itseumnikka?

(2) Terms of Social Import and Miscellaneous Words

family	home
가족	가정
gajok	*gajeong*

parents	children
부모님	자녀/아이들
bumonim	*janyeo/a-ideul*

son	daughter
아들	딸
adeul	*ttal*

father	mother
아버지	어머니
abeoji	*eomeoni*

grandfather	grandmother
할아버지	할머니
harabeoji	*halmeoni*

younger brother	elder brother
동생	형님
dongsaeng	*hyeongnim*

elder sister	nephew/nice
누님	조카
nunim	*joka*

hometown	friend
고향	친구
gohyang	*chin-gu*

friendship	marriage
우정	결혼
ujeong	*gyeolhon*
student	school/university
학생	학교/대학교
haksaeng	*hakgyo/daehakgyo*
major	(old) classmate
전공	동문/동기
jeon-gong	*dongmun/dong-gi*
occupation	mailing address
직업	주소
jigeop	*juso*
number	FAX
번호	팩스
beonho	*paekseu*
contact	memo
연락	메모지
yeollak	*memo(ji)*

pencil

연필

yeonpil

newspaper

신문

sinmun

magazine

잡지

japji

radio

라디오

radio

copying machine

복사기

boksagi

laundry

세탁소

setakso

pen

펜

pen

newspaper company

신문사

sinmunsa

television

텔레비전

tellebijeon

copy

복사

boksa

store

가게

gage

supermarket

슈퍼마켓

syupeomaket

3. Greetings

Greetings are a way to get started in a foreign language. After all, when you arrive, you'll want to say things like "Hello, my name is⋯, what's your name?" or "Hi, I'm a tourist, can you help me find my hotel?" Phrases like these will be found in this section. You can use these expressions throughout your trip, or even with your Korean friends. Besides being applicable all the time, these basic words and phrases will also be helpful with your pronunciation because they contain many of the most common sounds in the Korean language. Try to learn as many as you can.

Korean surnames are quite simple, usually consisting of one syllable, followed by the given name (note that this is the reverse of Western practice). Titles, such as Mr. and Mrs. will always follow the name rather than preceding them. We'll see examples of this sort in the following section.

How do you do?

처음 뵙겠습니다.

cheo-eum boepgetseumnida.

How are you (doing)?

안녕하세요?

annyeonghaseyo?

Good afternoon.

안녕하십니까?

annyeonghasimnikka?

Good evening.

안녕하십니까?

annyeonghasimnikka?

Good day.

안녕하십니까?

annyeonghasimnikka?

Good night.

안녕히 주무세요.

annyeonghi jumuseyo.

Glad(Pleased) to see(meet) you.

만나서 반갑습니다.

mannaseo ban-gapseumnida.

Hello.

_ 안녕하십니까?(for greeting)

annyeonghasimnikka?

_ 여보세요?(for phone call)

yeoboseyo?

Good bye!

안녕히 가세요.(to sb. leaving _____)

annyeonghi gaseyo.

See you later.

안녕히 계세요.

annyeonghi gyeseyo.

See you later.

나중에 봅시다.

najung-e bopsida.

Forget it.

잊으십시오.

ijeusipsio.

Never mind.

걱정 마십시오.

geokjeong masipsio.

This is Mr <u>Jang</u>.

이분은 <u>장선생님</u>입니다.

ibuneun <u>Jang seonsaengnim</u> imnida.

No problem.

문제없습니다.

munje-eopseumnida.

Hello, Mr. Kim?

김 선생님 안녕하세요?

Kim seonsaengnim annyeonghaseyo?

How are you today?

오늘은 어떠세요?

oneureun eotteoseyo?

Oh, I see.

아, 알겠습니다.

a, algetseumnida.

I'm fine, thanks.

잘 있습니다. 감사합니다.

jal itseumnida. gamsahamnida.

And you?

당신은 어떠세요?

dangsineun eotteoseyo?

Pretty good.

아주 좋습니다.

aju joseumnida.

Are you going shopping?

시장에 가려고 합니까?

sijang-e garyeogo hamnikka?

Yes, I am.

네, 그렇습니다.

ne, geureoseumnida.

It's almost time for lunch now.

이제 점심시간이군요.

ije jeomsimsiganigunyo.

See you later.(or Be seeing you)

다시 만납시다.

dasi mannapsida.

PART II
FOR
SIGHTSEEING
TRAVELERS

1. Before you leave for Korea

Don't go to Korea without any knowledge about the people you are going to meet.

It is important to know at least a little bit about the host country's culture. People everywhere like to be greeted by a foreigner in their own tongue. Do some study in advance about Korea when you are making plans to visit, not only her geography but also the socio-cultural background of the people.

(1) Who are you? and Where do you come from?

Where do you come from?

어디서 오셨습니까?

eodiseo osyeotseumnikka?

Who are you?

당신은 누구십니까?

dangsineun nugusimnikka?

I am <u>John</u>(your name).

저는 존입니다.

jeoneun <u>Jon</u> imnida.

Where do you come from?

어디 출신입니까?

eodi chulsinimnikka?

I come from the United States.

미국 출신입니다.

miguk chulsinimnida.

I come from England.

영국 출신입니다.

yeongguk chulsinimnida.

I come from Canada.

캐나다 출신입니다.

kaenada chulsinimnida.

What nationality are you?

국적은 어디십니까?

gukjeogeun eodisimnikka?

I am (an) American/Canadian.

저는 미국인/캐나다인입니다.

jeoneun migugin/kaenada-inimnida.

I am (an) Englishman/Australian.

저는 영국인/호주인입니다.

jeoneun yeonggugin/hojuinimnida.

What's your full name?

성함은요?

seonghameunyo?

My full name is John Smith.

저는 존 스미스입니다.

jeoneun jon seumiseu-imnida.

What's your surname(family name)?

당신의 성씨는 무엇입니까?

*dangsinui seongssineun
mu-eosimnikka?*

My surname is Kim.

제 성은 김(씨)입니다.

je seong-eun Kim(ssi)imnida.

What's your first name?

당신의 이름은 무엇입니까?

dangsinui ireumeun mu-eosimnikka?

My first name is John.

제 이름은 존입니다.

je ireumeun jonimnida.

(2) Whose is this? and Where is it?

Whose is this?

이것은 누구의 것입니까?

igeoseun nugu-ui geosimnikka?

That's mine.

그것은 제 것입니다.

geugeoseun je geosimnida.

It's ours.

그것은 우리들 것입니다.

geugeoseun urideul geosimnida.

Is it yours or not?

그것이 당신의 것입니까?

geugeosi dangsinui geosimnikka?

Is it his?

그것이 그의 것입니까?

geugeosi geu-ui geosimnikka?

No, it's not. It's mine.

아닙니다. 그것은 제 것입니다.

animnida. geugeoseun je geosimnida.

Where is <u>the station</u>?

<u>역</u>이 어디에 있습니까?

<u>yeok</u> i eodie itseumnikka?

Where is my luggage?

제 짐은 어디에 있습니까?

je jimeun eodie itseumnikka?

Where's the bathroom?

화장실은 어디에 있습니까?

hwajangsireun eodie itseumnikka?

Where's the restaurant?

식당은 어디에 있습니까?

sikdang-eun eodie itseumnikka?

(3) Here and There

It's here.

그것은 여기에 있습니다.

geugeoseun yeogie itseumnida.

It's there.

그것은 저기에 있습니다.

geugeoseun jeogie itseumnida.

It's on the left.

그것은 왼쪽에 있습니다.

geugeoseun oenjjoge itseumnida.

It's on the right.

그것은 오른쪽에 있습니다.

geugeoseun oreunjjoge itseumnida.

What is that?

저것은 무엇입니까?

jeogeoseun mu-eosimnikka?

That's my luggage.

그것은 제 짐입니다.

geugeoseun je jimimnida.

What do you want?

무엇을 원하십니까?

mu-eoseul wonhasimnikka?

I want to ask your help.

당신의 도움을 청하고 싶습니다.

dangsinui doumeul cheonghago sipseumnida.

When do we go?

언제 떠날까요?

eonje tteonalkkayo?

When will he come?

그가 언제 올까요?

geuga eonje olkkayo?

Which day?

무슨 요일에요?

museun yoireyo?

Today

오늘요.

oneuryo.

Which year?

어느 해에요?

eoneu hae-eyo?

Next year.

내년에요.

naenyeoneyo.

Which way?

어느 쪽에요?

eoneu jjogeyo?

This way, please.

이쪽입니다.

ijjogimnida.

Which one do you want?

어느 것을 원하십니까?

eoneu geoseul wonhasimnikka?

I want this one.

이것을 원합니다.

igeoseul wonhamnida.

Do you have (a) pencil?

연필(좀) 가지고 계십니까?

yeonpil(jom) gajigo gyesimnikka?

Yes, I have.

네, 가지고 있습니다.

ne, gajigo itseumnida.

No, I don't have (one).

아니요, 가지고 있지 않습니다.

aniyo, gajigo itji anseumnida.

Why did you come?

왜 오셨습니까?

wae osyeotseumnikka?

I've come to buy things.

물건 사러 왔습니다.

mulgeon sareo watseumnida.

That's correct.

맞습니다.

matseumnida.

How kind you are!

정말 친절하시군요.

jeongmal chinjeolhasigunyo.

Mr. Lee

미스터 리

miseuteo ri

Mrs. Kim

미세스 김

miseseu Kim

Miss. Go

미스 고

miseu go

Do you understand?

아시겠습니까?

asigetseumnikka?

Yes, I understand.

네, 알겠습니다.

ne, algetseumnida.

I don't understand.

모르겠습니다.

moreugetseumnida.

Do you know about it?

그것에 대해 아십니까?

geugeose daehae asimnikka?

I know.

압니다.

amnida.

I don't know.

모릅니다.

moreumnida.

Terrific!

> 정말 좋습니다.
>
> *jeongmal joseumnida.*

After you please.

> 먼저 가세요.
>
> *meonjeo gaseyo.*

Please help me.

> 도와주세요.
>
> *dowajuseyo.*

Thank you for helping me.

> 도와주셔서 감사합니다.
>
> *dowajusyeoseo gamsahamnida.*

Please wait for me.

> 기다려 주십시오.
>
> *gidaryeo jusipsio.*

Thank you for waiting for me.

> 기다려주셔서 감사합니다.
>
> *gidaryeojusyeoseo gamsahamnida.*

What a pity!

안됐군요.

andwaetgunyo.

Please hurry.

서두르십시오.

seodureusipsio.

Wait!

기다리십시오.

gidarisipsio.

Careful.

조심하세요.

josimhaseyo.

Please say it again.

다시 말씀해 주십시오.

dasi malsseumhae jusipsio.

Have a good trip!

여행 재미있게 하십시오.

yeohaeng jaemiitge hasipsio.

How have you been, Mr. Lee?

이 선생님 어떻게 지내셨습니까?

*iseonsaengnim eotteoke
jinaesyeotseumnikka?*

2. When you arrive

After a long trip, you arrive at the Incheon International Airport where customs officials await you. Passing through customs is a formality you'll want to finish quickly to start enjoying Korea. The phrases in this section are tailored to the particular set of terms and phrases used/heard around the customs inspection counter. Some customs officials in Korea speak good English, so if you have a problem, you'll be understood and helped promptly.

Your most important document during this part of your trip is the customs declaration form. On it you will itemize cameras, watches, jewelry and foreign currency taken into Korea. Keep the lists of your personal possessions, record and other reports, and currency (exchange vouchers, receipts for large purchases, and so forth).

(1) Passport Clearance

Here's my passport.

여기 제 여권이 있습니다.

yeogi je yeogwoni itseumnida.

My name is John.

제 이름은 존입니다.

je ireumeun jonimnida.

I'm <u>India</u>.

저는 <u>인도</u>사람입니다.

jeoneun <u>indo</u> saramimnida.

I'm Japanese.

저는 일본 사람입니다.

jeoneun ilbon saramimnida.

I'm Canadian.

저는 캐나다 사람입니다.

jeoneun kaenada saramimnida.

I'm British.

나는 영국 사람입니다.

naneun yeongguk saramimnida.

I'm Australian.

저는 호주 사람입니다.

jeoneun hoju saramimnida.

Could you tell me where the toilet is?

화장실이 어디에 있는지 말씀해 주시겠습
니까?

*hwajangsiri eodie inneunji
malsseumhae jusigetseumnikka?*

My address is <u>Sindang-dong</u>.

저의 주소는 <u>신당동</u> 입니다.

jeo-ui jusoneun <u>sindang-dong</u> imnida.

I'll be staying at the Hotel Lotte.

저는 롯데호텔에 머물려고 합니다.

*jeoneun rotdehotere meomul-
lyeogo hamnida.*

Here is(are) my passport.

저의 여권이 여기 있습니다.

jeo-ui yeogwoni yeogi itseumnida.

documents	passport
서류	여권
seoryu	*yeogwon*

health certificate

건강 증명서

geon-gang jeungmyeongseo

visa

입국사증

ipguk sajeung

I have come <u>on business</u>.

저는 <u>사업</u> 때문에 왔습니다.

jeoneun <u>sa-eop</u> ttaemune watseumnida.

on business

사업 때문에

sa-eop ttaemune

on vacation

휴가로

hyugaro

on a visit

방문하러

bangmunhareo

to visit relatives

친척을 찾아보려고

chincheogeul chajaboryeogo

I'm here with a group.

나는 일행이 있습니다.

naneun ilhaeng-i itseumnida.

I'll be staying <u>a week</u>.

저는 <u>일주일</u> 머물려고 합니다.

jeoneun <u>ilju-il</u> meomullyeogo hamnida.

a few days	a few weeks
며칠	몇 주
myeochil	*myeot ju*

a week	a month
일주일	한 달
ilju-il	*han dal*

with my husband

남편과 함께

nampyeon-gwa hamkke

alone	with my wife
혼자	아내와 함께
honja	*anaewa hamkke*

with my family

가족과 함께

gajokgwa hamkke

with my friend

친구와 함께

chin-guwa hamkke

with my colleague

동료와 함께

dongnyowa hamkke

with a tour group

관광일행과 함께

gwan-gwang-ilhaenggwa hamkke

(2) Customs

Have you anything to declare?

신고할 것이 있습니까?

sin-gohal geosi itseumnikka?

I don't have anything to declare.

신고할 것이 없습니다.

sin-gohal geosi eopseumnida.

I have to declare <u>medicine</u>.

<u>약</u>을 신고해야 합니다.

<u>*yak*</u> *eul sin-gohaeya hamnida.*

one camera	three bottles of medicine
카메라 하나	약 3병
kamera hana	*yak se byeong*
two watches	four pieces of jewelry
시계 둘	보석류 4개
sigye dul	*boseongnyu ne gae*

one carton of cigarettes

담배 한 박스

dambae han bakseu

one bottle of whisky

위스키 한 병

wiseuki han byeong

twenty rolls of film

필름 20통

pilleum isiptong

five hundred dollars of U.S. currency

미화 500불

mihwa obaekbul

Must I pay duty on this?

이것도 세금을 물어야 합니까?

igeotdo segeumeul mureoya hamnikka?

You must pay duty on this.

이것도 세금을 물어야 합니다.

igeotdo segeumeul mureoya hamnida.

How much?

얼마나요?

eolmanayo?

These are personal articles.

이것들은 제 개인소지품입니다.

igeotdeureun je gaeinsojipumimnida.

Please open this suitcase.

이 가방 좀 열어 주십시오.

i gabang jom yeoreo jusipsio.

Have you any more luggage?

짐이 더 있습니까?

jimi deo itseumnikka?

This is all I have.

이것이 모두입니다.

igeosi modu-imnida.

Where can I find an interpreter?

통역원이 있습니까?

tong-yeogwoni itseumnikka?

Please speak in English.

영어로 말해주세요.

yeong-eoro malhaejuseyo.

I want to make a telephone call.

전화 걸고 싶습니다.

jeonhwa geolgo sipseumnida.

Excuse me, porter!

여보세요, 아저씨.

yeoboseyo, ajeossi.

Please help me with my luggage.

짐 좀 운반해주세요.

jim jom unbanhaejuseyo.

Where is your luggage?

짐이 어디에 있습니까?

jimi eodie itseumnikka?

This is my luggage.

이것이 제 짐입니다.

igeosi je jimimnida.

Those are not mine.

이것들은 제 짐이 아닙니다.

igeotdeureun je jimi animnida.

That is mine.

저것이 제 것입니다.

jeogeosi je geosimnida.

I have five pieces of <u>luggages</u>.

저는 다섯 덩이의 <u>짐</u>이 있습니다.

jeoneun daseot deong-i-ui <u>jim</u> i itseumnida.

big luggages   small luggages

큰 짐들   작은 짐들

keun jimdeul   *jageun jimdeul*

blue luggages

푸른 색깔의 짐들

pureun saekkkarui jimdeul

black luggages

검은 색깔의 짐들

geomeun saekkkarui jimdeul

brown luggages

갈색의 짐들

galsaegui jimdeul

Those two pieces are also mine.

이 두 개의 짐도 저의 것입니다.

i du gae-ui jimdo jeo-ui geosimnida.

One piece is missing.

한 개가 없어졌습니다.

han gaega eopseojeotseumnida.

Is it this one?

이것입니까?

igeosimnikka?

Yes, that's mine.

네, 그것이 제 것입니다.

ne, geugeosi je geosimnida.

I've lost my luggage.

제 짐을 분실했습니다.

je jimeul bunsilhaetseumnida.

Can you help me find it?

찾는데 도와주시겠습니까?

channeunde dowajusigetseumnikka?

Where's the Lost and Found Office?

분실물 사무실이 어디에 있습니까?

bunsilmul samusiri eodie itseumnikka?

Please take these bags <u>outside</u>.

이 짐들을 <u>밖으로</u> 가져가세요.

i jimdeureul <u>bakkeuro</u> gajeogaseyo.

outside	inside
밖으로	안으로
bakkeuro	*aneuro*

to the taxi stand

택시 타는 곳으로

taeksi taneun goseuro

to the bus station

버스정거장으로

beoseujeong-geojang-euro

Where can I get a taxi?

어디에서 택시를 탈 수 있습니까?

eodieseo taeksireul tal su itseumnikka?

Where's the bus station?

버스정거장은 어디에 있습니까?

beoseujeong-geojang-eun eodie itseumnikka?

I want to go the Shilla hotel.

신라호텔로 가고 싶습니다.

silla hotello gago sipseumnida.

Thank you for your help.

도와주셔서 감사합니다.

dowajusyeoseo gamsahamnida.

(4) Transportation

taxi

택시

taeksi

car with driver

운전수 딸린 차

unjeonsu ttallin cha

bus(stop)

버스(정거장)

beoseu(jeong-geojang)

subway(station)

지하철(역)

jihacheol(yeok)

plane	airport
비행기	비행장
bihaenggi	*bihaengjang*

I'd like to go to the <u>silla</u> Hotel.

저는 <u>신라</u>호텔에 가고 싶습니다.

jeoneun <u>silla</u> hotere gago sipseumnida.

Lotte	Chosun
롯데	조선
rotde	*joseon*

Shilla	Hilton
신라	힐튼
silla	*hilteun*

Walker Hill	Sejong
워커힐	세종
wokeohil	*sejong*

Plaza	Ramada
플라자	라마다
peullaja	*ramada*

Where can I get a taxi?

어디서 택시를 탑니까?

eodiseo taeksireul tamnikka?

Please take me to this address.

이 주소로 좀 데려다 주십시오.

i jusoro jom deryeoda jusipsio.

I want to go to <u>Namdaemun market</u>.

<u>남대문 시장</u>에 가고 싶습니다.

<u>*namdaemun sijang*</u> *e gago sipseumnida.*

Namdaemun market

남대문 시장

namdaemun sijang

U.S. Embassy

미국 대사관

miguk daesagwan

Canada Embassy

캐나다 대사관

kaenada daesagwan

Australian Embassy

호주 대사관

hoju daesagwan

Stop here, at the corner, please.

여기 모퉁이에 세워주십시오.

yeogi motung-ie sewojusipsio.

Please wait for me.

좀 기다려주십시오.

jom gidaryeojusipsio.

I'll be right back.

곧 돌아오겠습니다.

got doraogetseumnida.

I have some baggage.

제가 짐이 있습니다.

jega jimi itseumnida.

Where is the nearest bus stop?

가장 가까운 버스정거장이 어디 있습니까?

gajang gakkaun beoseu jeong-geojang-i eodi itseumnikka?

Is there a subway map in English?

영어로 된 지하철지도가 있습니까?

yeong-eoro doen jihacheol jidoga itseumnikka?

Which line goes to <u>jongno</u>?

어느 노선이 <u>종로</u>에 갑니까?

eoneu noseoni <u>jongno</u> e gamnikka?

Does this bus go to <u>city hall</u>?

이 버스가 <u>시청</u>에 갑니까?

i beoseuga <u>sicheong</u> e gamnikka?

Cith Hall	Euljiro
시청	을지로
sicheong	*euljiro*
Jongno	Sejongno
종로	세종로
jongno	*sejongno*

Where should I get off for <u>Chosun hotel</u>?

조선호텔에 가려면 어디서 내립니까?

<u>josun hotel</u> e garyeomyeon eodiseo nae-rimnikka?

How many stops to <u>city hall</u>?

시청은/는 몇 번째 정거장입니까?

<u>sicheong</u> eun/neun myeot beonjjae jeong-geojang-imnikka?

I want to get off here.

여기서 내리고 싶습니다.

yeogiseo naerigo sipseumnida.

Please tell me when we get to <u>station</u>.

역에 도착하면 저에게 말씀해 주십시오.

<u>yeok</u> e dochakamyeon jeo-ege malsseumhae jusipsio.

How often do the buses run?

버스는 얼마나 자주 다닙니까?

beoseuneun eolmana jaju danimnikka?

3. At the Hotel

Staying at a hotel in Korea will give you many chances to use the Korean language. The hotel staff will be glad to help, although many of them will be equally interested in practicing their English on you. Why not trade some of your English for Korean? In general, hotels in Korea that serve foreigners are equipped with many practical facilities. Most are spacious enough and comfortable, containing the usual basic furniture, accessories and amenities. Most hotels have Western rooms, but some hotels have both Western and traditional Korean rooms with ondol floors heated by a system of radiant pipes.

Hotels are classified into four types according to size, facilities and quality of service. They use roses of Sharon, the national flower of Korea, as a symbol of quality. Five flowers indicate deluxe class, four first class, three second class, and two third class. Major international credit cards are accepted by most hotels. Besides hotels there are traditional Korean style inns called yeogwan with ondol floors. Accomodations and services are traditional, providing a more homelike atmosphere. You may easily find a comfortable yeogwan in cities and in the countryside alike. Although prices are relatively low compared to hotels, the yeogwan may appeal to those who wish to experience more of the local culture.

I have a reservation.

> 저는 예약을 했습니다.
>
> *jeoneun yeyageul haetseumnida.*

I need a room for one night.

> 저는 하룻밤 묵을 방이 필요합니다.
>
> *jeoneun harutbam mugeul bang-i piryohamnida.*

I want a double room with a bath.

> 저는 목욕탕이 있는 큰 방을 원합니다.
>
> *jeoneun mogyoktang-i inneun keun bang-eul wonhamnida.*

What is the rate for the room?

> 그 방값은 얼마입니까?
>
> *geu banggapseun eolma-imnikka?*

Where is th elevator?

> 엘리베이터가 어디에 있습니까?
>
> *ellibeiteoga eodie itseumnikka?*

Please wake me tomorrow at 7 o'clock.

내일 일곱 시에 깨워주십시오.

naeil ilgopsie kkaewojusipsio.

Did anyone call for me?

저한테 전화 온 것 있습니까?

jeohante jeonhwa on geot itseumnikka?

I'd like to put this in the hotel safe.

이것을 호텔보관함에 두고 싶습니다.

igeoseul hotelbogwanhame dugo sipseumnida.

Can you please make this call for me?

이 전화 좀 걸어주시겠습니까?

i jeonhwa jom georeojusigetseumnikka?

Please send someone up for the bags.

짐꾼 좀 올려 보내주십시오.

jimkkun jom ollyeo bonaejusipsio.

I'd like the bill, please.

계산서 좀 주십시오.

gyesanseo jom jusipsio.

Major Hotels in Seoul

Sofitel Ambassador

186-54, 2-ga, Jangchung-dong, Jung-gu

Grand Hyatt

747-7, Hannam-dong, Youngsan-gu

Sejong

61-3, 2-ga, Chungmu-ro, Jung-gu

Koreana

61, 1-ga, Taepyeong-ro, Jung-gu

Lotte

1, Sogong-dong, Jung-gu

President

188-3, 1-ga, Eulgi-ro, Jung-gu

Hilton

395, 5-ga, Namdaemun-ro, Jung-gu

Palace

63-1, Banpo-dong, Seocho-gu

Plaza

23, 2-ga, Taepyeong-ro, Jung-gu

Royal

6, 1-ga, Myeong-dong, Jung-gu

Sheraton Walkerhill

21, Gwangjang-dong, Gwangjin-gu

Shilla

202, 2-ga, Jangchung-dong, Jung-gu

(2) Making your flight reservation

When is there a flight to <u>India</u>?

인도행 비행기는 언제 있습니까?

<u>Indo</u> haeng bihaenggineun eonje itseumnikka?

Where do I pick up my luggage?

제 짐을 어디서 찾습니까?

je jimeul eodiseo chatseumnikka?

That flight has been delayed/cancelled.

그 비행기가 연착/취소됐습니다.

*geu bihaenggiga yeonchak/
chwisodwaetseumnida.*

May I carry this bag in the plane?

이 가방을 비행기에 가지고 타도 괜찮습니까?

*i gabang-eul bihaenggie gajigo
tado gwaenchanseumnikka?*

Your bags are overweight.

선생님의 가방무게가 초과되었습니다.

*seonsaengnimui gabangmugega
chogwadoeeotseumnida.*

I'd like a seat in the <u>window</u>.

나는 <u>창가</u>에 앉고 싶습니다.

naneun <u>changga</u> e ango sipseumnida.

nonsmoking section

금연석

geumyeonseok

smoking section

흡연석

heubyeonseok

near the window

창가

changga

on the aisle

통로 옆

tongno yeop

What time does the plane leave?

몇 시에 비행기가 떠납니까?

*myeot sie bihaenggiga
tteonamnikka?*

What's my flight number?

제 비행기(번호)는 몇 번입니까?

*je bihaenggi(beonho)neun myeot
beonimnikka?*

What's the gate number?

출구(번호)는 몇 번입니까?

*chulgu(beonho)neun myeot
beonimnikka?*

I'd like to confirm my flight reservaion.

제 비행기 예약을 확인하고 싶습니다.

*je bihaenggi yeyageul hwagin-
hago sipseumnida.*

(3) Renting a car

I would like to rent <u>a small car</u>.

저는 <u>작은차</u>를 빌리고 싶습니다.

jeoneun <u>jageun cha</u> reul billigo sipseumnida.

a car with automatic transmission

오토매틱 차

o-tomae-tik cha

a small car

작은 차 or 소형차

jageun cha or sohyeongcha

medium size car

중형차

junghyeongcha

How much does it cost per <u>week</u>.

> <u>일주일</u>에 얼마입니까?
>
> *<u>ilju-il</u> e eolma-imnikka?*

> day
>
> 하루
>
> *haru*

> week
>
> 일주일
>
> *ilju-il*

> kilometer
>
> 킬로당
>
> *killodang*

How much is the insurance?

> 보험료는 얼마입니까?
>
> *boheomnyoneun eolma-imnikka?*

Do you accept credit cards?

> 신용카드를 받습니까?
>
> *sinyongkadeureul batseumnikka?*

Do I have to leave a deposit?

> 보증금을 내야 합니까?
>
> *bojeunggeumeul naeya hamnikka?*

I want to rent the car here.

여기서 차를 빌리고 싶습니다.

yeogiseo chareul billigo sipseumnida.

I would like to leave it in some place else.

다른 곳에 두고 싶습니다.

dareun gose dugo sipseumnida.

Where is the gas station?

주유소가 어디에 있습니까?

juyusoga eodie itseumnikka?

Fill her up.

가득 넣어주세요.

gadeuk neo-eojuseyo.

Please check the <u>battery</u>.

<u>배터리</u> 을/를 좀 봐 주십시오.

<u>*baeteori*</u> *eul/reul jom bwa jusipsio.*

battery	hood
배터리	보닛
baeteori	*bonit*

carburetor

카뷰레터

kabyureteo

oil

오일

oil

spark plugs

스파크 플러그

seupakeu peulleogeu

tires

타이어

ta-ieo

water

물

mul

(4) Leisure Time Activities

Where can I buy <u>bread</u>.

어디서 <u>빵</u>을/를 살 수 있습니까?

eodiseo <u>ppang</u> eul/reul sal su itseumnikka?

an English newspaper

영자 신문

yeongja sinmun

ticket

표

pyo

staff

지팡이

jipang-i

cap

모자

moja

rope

로프

ropeu

dust bin

쓰레기통

sseuregitong

I'd like to see <u>folk village</u>.

<u>민속촌</u>을/를 보고 싶습니다.

<u>*minsokchon*</u> *eul/reul bogo sipseumnida.*

a baseball game

야구시합

yagusihap

folk village

민속촌

minsokchon

Panmunjeom

판문점

panmunjeom

Gyeongbokgung

경복궁

gyeongbokgung

Where can I buy the tickets?

표를 어디서 살 수 있습니까?

pyoreul eodiseo sal su itseumnikka?

Is there a pool near the hotel?

호텔 근처에 수영장이 있습니까?

hotel geuncheo-e suyeongjang-i itseumnikka?

Is it far from here?

멉니까?

meomnikka?

Is there a discotheque here?

이 근처에 디스코클럽이 있습니까?

i geuncheo-e diseuko keulleobi itseumnikka?

Is there one at the hotel?

이 호텔에 있습니까?

i hotere itseumnikka?

I would like to reserve a table.

자리를 예약하고 싶습니다.

jarireul yeyakago sipseumnida.

Where is the nearest pharmacy?

가까운 약국이 어디 있습니까?

gakkaun yakgugi eodi itseumnikka?

Is there a pharmacy that carries American medicine?

미제 약을 파는 약국이 있습니까?

mije yageul paneun yakgugi itseumnikka?

I need something for <u>constipation</u>.

나는 <u>변비</u>약이 필요합니다.

naneun <u>byeonbi</u> yagi piryohamnida.

a cold	indigestion
감기	소화불량
gamgi	*sohwabullyang*
constipation	insomnia
변비	불면증
byeonbi	*bulmyeonjeung*

a cough

기침

gichim

a toothache

치통

chitong

diarrhea

설사

seolsa

an upset stomach

위통

witong

a headache

두통

dutong

I don't feel well.

몸이 좀 불편합니다.

momi jom bulpyeonhamnida.

I need a doctor who speaks English.

영어를 할 수 있는 의사가 필요합니다.

yeong-eoreul hal su inneun uisaga piryohamnida.

I'm dizzy.

어지럽습니다.

eojireopseumnida.

I feel weak.

기운이 없습니다.

giuni eopseumnida.

I have a pain in my chest around my heart.

심장 부근 가슴이 아픕니다.

simjang bugeun gaseumi apeumnida.

I had a heart attack some years ago.

몇 년 전 심장마비에 걸렸었습니다.

myeot nyeon jeon simjangmabie geollyeosseotseumnida.

I'm taking this medicine.

이 약을 쓰고 있습니다.

i yageul sseugo itseumnida.

Do I have to go to the hospital?

병원에 가야 합니까?

byeong-wone gaya hamnikka?

I have a toothache.

치통이 있습니다.

chitong-i itseumnida.

Could you recommend a dentist?

치과의사를 소개해 주시겠습니까?

chigwa-uisareul sogaehae jusigetseumnikka?

I just broke my glasses.

제 안경이 방금 깨졌습니다.

je an-gyeong-i banggeum kkaejeotseumnida.

Can you repair them while I wait?

기다리는 동안 고쳐 주실 수 있습니까?

gidarineun dong-an gocheo jusil su itseumnikka?

(6) Telephone Conversation

You are wanted on the phone.

전화 왔어요.

jeonhwa wasseoyo.

Hello. who is this?

여보세요. 누구세요?

yeoboseyo. nuguseyo?

This is <u>chef</u>.

저는 <u>주방장</u>입니다.

jeoneun <u>jubangjang</u> imnida.

May I speak with <u>front</u>?

<u>프론트</u>와 통화할 수 있습니까?

<u>peuronteu</u> wa tonghwahal su itseumnikka?

Hello. I want 555-1111 please.

여보세요. 오오오의 일일일일번 좀 부탁합
니다.

yeoboseyo. o-o-o-ui il-il-il-ilbeon jom butakamnida.

Hello. Please connect me with the Lotte Hotel.

여보세요. 롯데호텔 좀 연결해주세요.

yeoboseyo. rotdehotel jom yeon-gyeolhae juseyo.

I'm sorry, the line is busy.

죄송합니다만, 통화중입니다.

*joesonghamnidaman, tonghwajung-
imnida.*

No one answers.

전화 받지 않습니다.

jeonhwa batji anseumnida.

Thanks, I'll try again later.

감사합니다. 나중에 걸겠습니다.

*gamsahamnida. najung-e
geolgetseumnida.*

Please give him a message.

내용 좀 전해주세요.

naeyong jom jeonhaejuseyo.

Operator, I dialed the wrong number.

교환, 번호를 잘못 돌렸습니다.

*gyohwan beonhoreul jalmot
dollyeotseumnida.*

I can't speak Korean.

저는 한국어를 못합니다.

jeoneun han-gugeoreul motamnida.

Please speak English.

영어로 좀 말해주세요.

yeong-eoro jom malhaejuseyo.

Where there any calls for me?

저에게 전화 온 것이 있습니까?

jeo-ege jeonhwa on geosi itseumnikka?

Yes, Mr. Kim called.

네, 김씨가 전화했습니다.

ne, gimssiga jeonhwahaetseumnida.

Here's his telephone number.

여기 그의 전화번호가 있습니다.

yeogi geu-ui jeonhwabeonhoga itseumnida.

The telephone is out of order.

전화기가 고장 났습니다.

jeonhwagiga gojang natseumnida.

May I have a telephone directory?

전화번호부 좀 볼까요?

jeonhwabeonhobu jom bolkkayo?

I want to call my home.

집에 전화하고 싶습니다.

jibe jeonhwahago sipseumnida.

What time is it in the United States now?

미국에서는 지금 몇 시죠?

migugeseoneun jigeum myeot sijyo?

Where is a public telephone?

공중전화가 어디에 있습니까?

gongjungjeonhwaga eodie itseumnikka?

Is there an English telephone directory?

영어로 된 전화번호부가 있습니까?

yeong-eoro doen jeonhwabeonhobu-ga itseumnikka?

I'd like to make a phone call.

전화를 걸려고 합니다.

jeonhwareul geollyeogo hamnida.

May I use your phone?

댁의 전화 좀 써도 괜찮습니까?

daegui jeonhwa jom sseodo gwaenchanseumnikka?

How do you call the United States?

미국에 어떻게 전화합니까?

miguge eotteoke jeonhwa-hamnikka?

How do you call Canada?

캐나다에 어떻게 전화합니까?

kaenada-e eotteoke jeonhwa-hamnikka?

How do you call Australia?

호주에 어떻게 전화합니까?

hoju-e eotteoke jeonhwahamnikka?

How do you call England?

영국에 어떻게 전화합니까?

yeongguge eotteoke jeonhwa-hamnikka?

I'd like to talk to the operator.

교환과 통화하고 싶습니다.

gyohwan-gwa tonghwahago sipseumnida.

May I speak to <u>manager</u>?

<u>지배인</u>좀 타꾸어 주시겠습니까?

<u>*jibaein*</u> *jom bakku-eo jusigetseumnikka?*

Who's calling?

누구십니까?

nugusimnikka?

Speak slowly, please.

천천히 말씀해 주십시오.

cheoncheonhi malsseumhae jusipsio.

Speak louder please.

크게 말씀해 주십시오.

keuge malsseumhae jusipsio.

Don't hang up.

끊지 마십시오.

kkeunchi masipsio.

I got a wrong number.

잘못 걸었습니다.

jalmot georeotseumnida.

I was disconnected.

연결이 안 됐습니다.

yeon-gyeori an dwaetseumnida.

I would like to leave a message.

말씀 좀 전해 주시겠습니까?

malsseum jom jeonhae jusigetseumnikka?

He/She isn't here.

그분이 여기 안 계십니다.

geubuni yeogi an gyesimnida.

The line is busy.

통화 중입니다.

tonghwa jung-imnida.

He/She'll be back at <u>7 o'clock</u>.

그분은 <u>7시</u>에 돌아오십니다.

geubuneun <u>ilgop-si</u> e doraosimnida.

He's <u>on vacation</u>.

그분은 <u>휴가중</u>입니다.

geubuneun <u>hyuga jung</u> imnida.

in a meeting	out to lunch
회의 중	점심식사 중
hoe-ui jung	*jeomsimsiksa jung*

on vacation

휴가 중

hyuga jung

mailbox

우체통

uchetong

letter

편지

pyeonji

post card

엽서

yeopseo

special delivery letter

속달편지

sokdal pyeonji

post office

우체국

ucheguk

air-mail letter

항공편지

hanggong pyeonji

registered letter

등기편지

deunggi pyeonji

Where is a mailbox?

우체통이 어디에 있습니까?

uchetong-i eodie itseumnikka?

I'd like to buy some stamps.

나는 우표를 사려고 합니다.

naneun upyoreul saryeogo hamnida.

Which window is it?

어느 창구입니까?

eoneu changgu-imnikka?

What's the postage to the United States?

미국까지 우편요금은 얼마입니까?

miguk-kkaji upyeon-yogeumeun eolma-imnikka?

How late are you open?

몇 시까지 엽니까?

myeot si-kkaji yeomnikka?

4. Dining

Koreans are not accustomed to eating while driving or walking along the street. However making food is one of the glories of Korean culture and one you can delight daily. Breakfast, lunch, and dinner times in Korea are similar to customs almost everywhere else. Visitors to Korea often eat at assigned tables from a specially prepared hotel menu. If you have special dietary needs or are allergic to certain kinds of food, make your requests in advance for help. Make a list of the foods that don't agree with you and try to learn to say them in Korea. Here is a handy guide.

I can't eat _____.

저는 _____을 먹지 못합니다.

jeoneun _____eul meokji motamnida.

Often at the table you will be given chopsticks. Don't worry though, because knives and forks also are always available.

Restaurants abound in Korea. One is never far away. Eating establishments vary from fast food ramyeon and coffee shops to buffet in large cities. There are many menus to choose from. Some different regions specialize in their own traditional foods. For example, hanjeongsik or bibimbap is well known for its various kinds.

Don't expect to be able to make a reservation at every restaurant. Generally, only first-rate restaurants will accept reservations. Be prepared to wait more than 20 minutes for a table at a popular restaurant.

Alcholic beverages are not so expensive as in western countries. Tipping is not customary in restaurants. Bars and discotheques serve alcohol but no regular food. However, they stay open until midnight.

(1) At a Hotel Restaurant

Is there a restaurant in the hotel?

호텔에 식당이 있습니까?

hotere sikdang-i itseumnikka?

Yes, there is.

예, 있습니다.

ye, itseumnida.

What floor is it on?

몇 층에 있습니까?

myeot cheung-e itseumnikka?

It's on the third floor.

3층에 있습니다.

samcheung-e itseumnida.

What time do we eat dinner?

몇 시에 저녁을 먹습니까?

myeot sie jeonyeogeul meokseumnikka?

We eat dinner at six.

여섯시에 저녁을 먹습니다.

yeoseotsie jeonyeogeul meokseumnida.

Are you hungry?

배고프십니까?

baegopeusimnikka?

Very hungry.

매우 배고픕니다.

mae-u baegopeumnida.

(2) Eating out

Where are we going to eat?

어디에서 먹나요?

eodieseo meongnayo?

Let's eat out tonight.

오늘 저녁 외식합시다.

oneul jeonyeok oesikapsida.

Where is a good restaurant?

유명한 식당이 어디에 있습니까?

yu-myeonghan sikdang-i eodie itseumnikka?

What's it called?

이름이 무엇입니까?

ireumi mu-eosimnikka?

It's called <u>chungmu</u>.

이름은 <u>충무</u>입니다.

ireumeun <u>chungmu</u> imnida.

Is it far from here?

여기서 먼가요?

yeogiseo meon-gayo?

No, it's very close.

아니요, 매우 가까이 있습니다.

aniyo, mae-u gakka-i itseumnida.

What sort of food do they serve?

어떤 음식이 나오나요?

eotteon eumsigi naonayo?

They serve various kind of food.

여러 종류의 음식이 있습니다.

yeoreo jongnyu-ui eumsigi itseumnida.

Please call a taxi for us.

택시 좀 불러주세요.

taeksi jom bulleojuseyo.

Can you help me find a restaurant?

음식점 좀 찾아주세요.

eumsikjeom jom chajajuseyo.

I want to reserve a table.

테이블을 예약하고 싶습니다.

teibeureul yeyakago sipseumnida.

What time are you coming?

몇 시에 오시겠습니까?

myeot sie osigetseumnikka?

We'll arrive at six.

6시에 오겠습니다.

yeoseossie ogetseumnida.

How many altogether?

모두 몇 명입니까?

modu myeot myeong-imnikka?

Altogether there will be ten people.

모두 열 명입니다.

modu yeol myeong-imnida.

How much per person?

1인당 얼마입니까?

irindang eolma-imnikka?

10,000 won per person for <u>lunch</u>.

<u>점심식사</u>먹는 데 1인당 만 원입니다.

<u>Jeomsimsiksa</u> meongneun de irindang man wonimnida.

breakfast

아침식사

achimsiksa

lunch

점심식사

jeomsimsiksa

dinner

저녁식사

jeonyeoksiksa

Korean food

한식

hansik

Chinese food

중국음식

junggugeumsik

Japanese food

일식

ilsik

Western food

양식

yangsik

Korean restaurant

한식집

hansikjip

Chinese restaurant

중국집

junggukjip

Japanese restaurant

일식집

ilsikjip

Western restaurant

양식집

yangsikjip

Do you know a good restaurant?

좋은 음식점을 아십니까?

joeun eumsikjeomeul asimnikka?

Is it very expensive?

매우 비쌉니까?

mae-u bissamnikka?

Waiter!/Waitress!

웨이터/웨이트레스

weiteo/weiteureseu

We'd like to have lunch.

점심 먹고 싶습니다.

jeomsim meokgo sipseumnida.

I'd like to try Korean food.

한식을 먹어보고 싶습니다.

hansigeul meogeobogo sipseumnida.

The menu, please.

메뉴 좀 주십시오.

menyu jom jusipsio.

What's today's special?

오늘 특식은 무엇입니까?

oneul teuksigeun mu-eosimnikka?

What do you recommend?

무슨 음식을 권하시겠습니까?

museun eumsigeul
gwonhasigetseumnikka?

To begin with, please bring us a cocktail.

먼저 칵테일 좀 가져다주십시오.

meonjeo kakteil jom gajeodajusipsio.

a bottle of mineral water

미네랄 워터 한 병

mineral woteo han byeong

a beer

맥주 한 병

maekju han byeong

Do you have grape wine?

포도주 있습니까?

podoju itseumnikka?

I'd like to order now.

지금 주문하고 싶습니다.

jigeum jumunhago sipseumnida.

Show me the menu again, please.

메뉴 좀 다시 보여주십시오.

menyu jom dasi boyeojusipsio.

I'd like some coffee, please.

커피 좀 주십시오.

keopi jom jusipsio.

Do you have American cigarettes?

미국담배 있습니까?

migukdambae itseumnikka?

Please give me a lighter also.

라이터도 좀 주십시오.

ra-iteodo jom jusipsio.

Do you mind if I smoke?

담배 피워도 괜찮습니까?

dambae piwodo gwaenchanseumnikka?

Check, please.

계산서 좀 주십시오.

gyesanseo jom jusipsio.

Do you take <u>credit cards</u>?

<u>신용카드</u>을/를 받습니까?

<u>*sinyong kadeu*</u> *eul/reul batseumnikka?*

credit cards	traveller's checks
신용카드	여행자 수표
sinyong kadeu	*yeohaengja supyo*

Which credit cards do you take?

어떤 신용카드를 받습니까?

eotteon sinyong kadeureul batseumnikka?

Are the tax and service charge included?

세금과 서비스가 포함됐습니까?

*segeumgwa seobiseuga
pohamdwaetseumnikka?*

Is this correct?

이것이 맞습니까?

igeosi matseumnikka?

May I have a receipt, please?

영수증 좀 주시겠어요?

yeongsujeung jom jusigesseoyo?

We don't have much time.

우리는 시간이 없습니다.

urineun sigani eopseumnida.

Where are the restrooms?

화장실이 어디에 있습니까?

hwajangsiri eodie itseumnikka?

Could you bring me <u>a cup</u> please?

<u>컵</u> 좀 가져다주시겠습니까?

<u>*keop*</u> *jom gajeodajusigetseumnikka?*

a knife

칼

kal

a spoon

숟가락

sutgarak

a table spoon

찻숟가락

chatsutgarak

a saucer

잔 받침대

jan batchimdae

a glass

잔

jan

a plate

접시

jeopsi

a cup

컵

keop

a bowl

그릇

geureut

a napkin

냅킨

naepkin

a toothpick

이쑤시개

issusigae

an ashtray

재떨이

jaetteori

(3) To the waiter

I want to eat with chopsticks.

> 젓가락을 가지고 먹고 싶습니다.

> *jeotgarageul gajigo meokgo sipseumnida.*

Please show me how to hold the chopsticks.

> 젓가락 집는 방법 좀 알려주십시오.

> *jeotgarak jimneun bangbeop jom allyeojusipsio.*

I can't use chopsticks.

> 저는 젓가락을 사용할 수 없습니다.

> *jeoneun jeotgarageul sayonghal su eopseumnida.*

Please give me a knife and fork.

나이프와 포크 좀 주십시오.

na-ipeuwa pokeu jom jusipsio.

(4) Different Dishes

pork

돼지고기

dwaejigogi

soup

수프

supeu

beef

쇠고기

soegogi

chicken

닭고기

dakgogi

fish

생선

saengseon

shrimp

새우

saeu

vegetable

채소

chaeso

noodles

국수

guksu

Please bring me _____.

_____좀 주십시오.

_____jom jusipsio.

a glass of water	a bottle of wine
물 한 잔	술 한 병
mul han jan	*sul han byeong*
a knife	a pair of chopsticks
나이프 하나	젓가락 한 쌍
na-ipeu hana	*jeotgarak han ssang*
a fork	a dish
포크 하나	그릇 하나
pokeu hana	*geureut hana*
a spoon	two bottles of beer
스푼	맥주 두 병
seupun	*maekju du byeong*
a glass	bread
유리잔 하나	빵
yurijan hana	*ppang*

a napkin

냅킨

naepkin

an ashtray

재떨이

jaetteori

a bowl

주발

jubal

some sugar

설탕

seoltang

some pepper

후추

huchu

some hot pepper

좀 매운 후추

jom maeun huchu

two cups of coffee

커피 두 잔

keopi du jan

(5) If there is a problem

I can't eat, please take it away.

먹을 수 없으니 치워주세요.

meogeul su eopseuni chiwojuseyo.

We have ordered the wrong food.

음식을 잘못 시켰습니다.

eumsigeul jalmot sikyeotseumnida.

We would like to order some more food.

음식을 좀 더 시키고 싶습니다.

eumsigeul jom deo sikigo sipseumnida.

I don't like this.

저는 이것을 좋아하지 않습니다.

jeoneun igeoseul joahaji anseumnida.

I'm allergic to <u>beans</u>.

저는 <u>콩</u>에 알레르기가 있습니다.

jeoneun <u>kong</u> e allereugiga itseumnida.

Does this dish contain <u>garlic</u>?

이 음식에 <u>마늘</u>이 들었습니까?

i eumsige <u>maneul</u> i deureotseumnikka?

There is a mistake on the bill.

계산서가 잘못되었습니다.

gyesanseoga jalmotdoe-eotseumnida.

Please check it over.

다시 한 번 확인해 주십시오.

dasi han beon hwaginhae jusipsio.

May I speak to the manager?

지배인에게 말씀해 드릴까요?

jibaeinege malsseumhae deurilkkayo?

Do you accept personal checks?

자기앞 수표도 받습니까?

jagiap supyodo batseumnikka?

May I pay with a traveller's check?

여행자 수표로 지불해도 되나요?

yeohaengja supyoro jibulhaedo doenayo?

Where do we pay?

어디서 지불하나요?

eodiseo jibulhanayo?

I'm full.

저는 배가 부른데요.

jeoneun baega bureundeyo.

I've had enough.

많이 먹었습니다.

mani meogeotseumnida.

(6) Common Foods

1) Meats

beef	lamb
쇠고기	양고기
soegogi	*yanggogi*
chicken	ham
닭고기	햄
dakgogi	*haem*
duck	pork
오리고기	돼지고기
origogi	*dwaejigogi*

steak	sausage
스테이크	소시지
seuteikeu	*sosiji*
spare ribs	hamburger
갈비	햄버거
galbi	*haembeogeo*
roasted	cooked rare(underdone)
구운	설익은
guun	*seorigeun*
cooked medium	cooked well-done
반쯤 익은	잘 익은
banjjeum igeun	*jarigeun*
fried	tough
튀긴	질긴
twigin	*jilgin*
tender	
연한	
yeonhan	

2) Vegetables

rice(plain, boiled)	fried rice
밥	비빔밥
bap	*bibimbap*
potatoes	sweet potatoes
감자	고구마
gamja	*goguma*
beans	mushrooms
콩	버섯
kong	*beoseot*
onions	cucumber
양파	오이
yangpa	*o-i*
tomatoes	garlic
토마토	마늘
tomato	*maneul*

3) Fruits

orange	**lemon**
오렌지	레몬
orenji	*remon*
apple	**each**
사과	복숭아
sagwa	*boksung-a*
pear	**melon**
배	멜론
bae	*mellon*
banana	
바나나	
banana	

4) Desserts

ice cream	**fruit**
아이스크림	과일
aiseukeurim	*gwa-il*

cookies	crackers
과자	크래커
gwaja	*keuraekeo*
candy	pudding
캔디	푸딩
kaendi	*puding*
cake	sweets
케이크	사탕
keikeu	*satang*

5) Drinks

(boiled)water	brandy
(끓인)물	브랜디
(kkeurin)mul	*beuraendi*
tea	whisky
차	위스키
cha	*wiseuki*
coffee	beer
커피	맥주
keopi	*maekju*

lemonade

레몬주스
remonjuseu

orange juice

오렌지주스
orenjijuseu

milk

우유
uyu

green tea

녹차
nokcha

black tea

흑차
heukcha

6) Miscellaneous

soy sauce

간장
ganjang

cheese

치즈
chijeu

sugar

설탕
seoltang

butter

버터
beoteo

mustard

겨자
gyeoja

hungry

목마른
mongmareun

bill	men's room
청구서	남자화장실
cheongguseo	*namjahwajangsil*
menu	chopsticks
메뉴	젓가락
menyu	*jeotgarak*
tea spoon	waiter/waitress
찻숟갈	웨이터/웨이트리스
chatsutgal	*weiteo/weiteuriseu*
knife	soup spoon
칼	국자
kal	*gukja*
fork	spoon
포크	스푼
pokeu	*seupun*
a glass of	a bottle of _____
한 잔의	한 병의_____
han janui	*han byeong-ui_____*

snack shop	food store
간이식당	식료품점
ganisikdang	*singnyopumjeom*
snacks	restaurant
스낵	식당
seunaek	*sikdang*
dining hall	breakfast
연회실	아침
yeonhoesil	*achim*
lunch	dinner
점심	저녁
jeomsim	*jeonyeok*
tasty	salt
맛있는	소금
masinneun	*sogeum*
pepper	vinegar
후추	식초
huchu	*sikcho*

oil

기름

gireum

7) Tastes

hot(peppery)	salty
매운	짠
maeun	*jjan*
sweet	bitter
단	쓴
dan	*sseun*
sour	
신	
sin	

5. Shopping

In the capital of Seoul, one of the most popular places for foreigners to shop is Itaeweon near the U.S. Army base in Yongsan. Insadong and Myeongdong are also popular. There the prices are somewhat higher than at other local markets, but you can haggle or bargain over prices. Most downtown stores are open from 10.00 A.M. and remain open as late as midnight almost every day.

Besides department stores, there are various kinds of shopping places such as arcades, specialized shopping districts, open air markets, and duty-free shops for foreign tourists and shoppers.

(1) Useful Expressions

I want to go shopping.

쇼핑하고 싶습니다.

syopinghago sipseumnida.

What do you want to buy?

무엇을 사려고 하십니까?

mu-eoseul saryeogo hasimnikka?

I want to buy <u>hat</u>.

저는 <u>모자</u>를 사고 싶습니다.

jeoneun <u>moja</u> reul sago sipseumnida.

a painting	a rug
그림	양탄자
geurim	*yangtanja*
a piece of pottery	a piece of jewelry
도자기	보석류
dojagi	*boseongnyu*
an antique	a silk tie
골동품	실크타이
goldongpum	*silkeutai*
a silk scarf	a pair of shoes
실크스카프	구두
silkeuseukapeu	*gudu*
rice wine	a pair of socks
쌀 막걸리	양말
ssalmakgeolli	*yangmal*

a book

책
chaek

perfume

향수
hyangsu

a woolen sweater

털스웨터
teolseuweteo

a blouse

블라우스
beullauseu

a hat

모자
moja

underwear

속내의
songnae-ui

an overcoat

외투
oetu

What time do the stores open?

몇 시에 상점이 문을 엽니까?
*myeot sie sangjeomi muneul
yeomnikka?*

The stores open at nine.

저 상점은 9시에 문을 엽니다.
*jeo sangjeomeun ahopshie muneul
yeomnida.*

What time do the stores close?

몇 시에 상점이 문을 닫습니까?

myeot sie sangjeomi muneul datseumnikka?

They close at seven.

상점들이 7시에 문을 닫습니다.

sangjeomdeuri ilgopsie muneul datseumnida.

Where do foreigners shop?

외국인들은 어디서 쇼핑합니까?

oegugindeureun eodiseo syopinghamnikka?

Foreigners can shop at Itaeweon.

외국인들은 이태원에서 쇼핑할 수 있습니다.

oegugindeureun itaewoneseo syopinghal su itseumnida.

Insa-dong	Myeong-dong
인사동	명동
insadong	*myeongdong*

Is it far?

거리가 먼가요?

georiga meon-gayo?

No, It's nearby.

아니요, 가까이에 있습니다.

aniyo, gakkaie itseumnida.

How can I get there?

어떻게 갈 수 있습니까?

eotteoke gal su itseumnikka?

You can walk or go by taxi.

걸어서 가거나 택시로 갈 수 있습니다.

georeoseo gageona taeksiro gal su itseumnida.

You can take a bus.

버스 타고 갈 수 있습니다.

beoseu tago gal su itseumnida.

How much is it?

그것은 얼마입니까?

geugeoseun eolma-imnikka?

Where can I find <u>purse</u>?

지갑을/를 어디서 찾을 수 있습니까?
jigap eul/reul eodiseo chajeul su itseumnikka?

Can you help me?

좀 도와주실 수 있습니까?

jom dowajusil su itseumnikka?

I need <u>handbag</u>.

손가방이/가 필요합니다.

son-gabang i/ga piryohamnida.

Do you have any others?

다른 것이 있습니까?

dareun geosi itseumnikka?

Do you have anything <u>smaller</u>?

더 작은 것이 있습니까?
deo jageun geosi itseumnikka?

smaller	larger
더 작은	더 큰
deo jageun	*deo keun*

yellow

노란색의
noransaegui

red

붉은색의
bulgeunsaegui

Can I pay with a traveler's check?

여행자 수표를 드려도 됩니까?

yeohaengja supyoreul deuryeodo
doemnikka?

(2) Shops and Stores

I would like to go to <u>market</u>.

<u>시장</u>에 가고 싶습니다.

<u>sijang</u> e gago sipseumnida.

store

가게
gage

barber shop

이발소
ibalso

market

시장
sijang

beauty parlor

미장원
mijangwon

department store
백화점
baekhwajeom

bakery
제과점
jegwajeom

shoe store
양화점
yanghwajeom

tailor shop
양복점
yangbokjeom

dressmaking store
양장점
yangjangjeom

street stall
노점
nojeom

stationery
문방구
munbanggu

souvenir store
기념품가게
ginyeompumgage

book store
책방
chaekbang

gas station
주유소
juyuso

florist
꽃가게
kkotgage

antique store
골동품점
goldongpumjeom

tobacco store

담뱃가게

dambaetgage

laundry

세탁소

setakso

general store

잡화점

japhwajeom

Do you want to drop in <u>florist</u>?

꽃가게에 들리고 싶습니까?

<u>kkotgage</u> e deulligo sipseumnikka?

How much is it?

그것은 얼마입니까?

geugeoseun eolma-imnikka?

Where can I find <u>book store</u>?

서점을/를 어디서 찾을 수 있습니까?

<u>seo jeom</u> eul/reul eodiseo chajeul su itseumnikka?

Can you help me?

좀 도와주실 수 있습니까?

jom dowajusil su itseumnikka?

I need <u>antique</u>.

골동품이 있습니까?

goldongpum i itseumnikka?

Do you have any others?

다른 것이 있습니까?

dareun geosi itseumnikka?

Do you have anything <u>larger</u>?

더 큰 것이 필요합니까?

deo keun geosi piryohamnikka?

Hello. I am a foreigner.

여보세요. 저는 외국사람입니다.
*yeoboseyo. jeoneun oeguksaram
imnida.*

Can you help me?

도와주시겠어요?
dowajusigesseoyo?

Are you the salesperson?

당신은 판매원입니까?
dangsineun panmaewonimnikka?

Welcome. what do you wish to buy?

어서오세요. 무엇을 사려고 합니까?

eoseooseyo. mu-eoseul saryeogo hamnikka?

Do you have any <u>book</u>?

<u>책</u>을 가지고 있습니까?

<u>*chack*</u> *eul gajigo itseumnikka?*

(3) About Prices

How much is this?

이것은 얼마입니까?
igeoseun eolma-imnikka?

That costs <u>ten thousand</u> won.

그것은 <u>만 원</u>입니다.
geugeoseun <u>man won</u> imnida.

five thousand won

오천 원
ocheon won

ten thousand won

만 원

man won

That's too expensive.

그것은 너무 비쌉니다.

geugeoseun neomu bissamnida.

I don't like this color.

이 색깔은 마음에 들지 않습니다.

i saekkkareun maeume deulji anseumnida.

I don't like this style.

이 스타일은 마음에 들지 않습니다.

i seuta-ireun maeume deulji anseumnida.

This is the wrong size.

사이즈가 틀립니다.

sa-ijeuga teullimnida.

I'd like to see another.

다른 것 좀 보고 싶습니다.

dareun geot jom bogo sipseumnida.

Please show me a <u>smaller size</u>.

<u>작은 사이즈</u> 좀 보여주십시오.

<u>*jageun sa-ijeu*</u> *jom boyeojusipsio.*

larger size

보다 큰 사이즈

boda keun sa-ijeu

smaller size

보다 작은 사이즈

boda jageun sa-ijeu

cheaper one

보다 값이 싼 것

boda gapsi ssan geot

Please take my measurements.

재어주세요.

jae-eojuseyo.

What size shoes do you wear?

몇 사이즈 크기의 구두를 신나요?
myeot sa-ijeu keugi-ui gudureul sinnayo?

I wear size seven.

사이즈 7을 신습니다.
sa-ijeu chireul sinseumnida.

This is too small.

이것은 너무 작습니다.
igeoseun neomu jakseumnida.

This is too big.

이것은 너무 큽니다.
igeoseun neomu keumnida.

(4) Buying a Gift

I want to buy a gift for <u>my wife</u>.

나는 <u>아내</u>에게 줄 선물을 사고 싶습니다.
naneun <u>anae</u> ege jul seonmureul sago sipseumnida.

my friend

나의 친구

naui chin-gu

my wife

나의 아내

naui anae

my husband

나의 남편

naui nampyeon

a child

아기

agi

I want a <u>blue</u> one.

나는 푸른것을 원합니다.

naneun <u>pureun</u> geoseul wonhamnida.

blue

푸른

pureun

yellow

노란색의

noransaegui

black

검은

geomeun

pink

핑크색의

pingkeusaegui

brown

갈색의

galsaegui

gray

회색의

hoesaegui

green	bright colored
초록의	밝은 색의
chorogui	*balgeun saegui*
white	dark colored
흰색의	짙은 색의
huinsaegui	*jiteun saegui*
red	bright red
붉은색의	선홍색의
bulgeunsaegui	*seonhongsaegui*
larger	smaller
보다 큰	보다 작은
boda keun	*boda jageun*

another(different one)

다른

dareun

This is too <u>wide</u>.

이것은 너무 <u>넓습니다</u>.

igeoseun neomu <u>neolseumnida</u>.

long	short
긴	짧은
gin	*jjalbeun*

wide	narrow
넓은	좁은
neolbeun	*jobeun*

small	large
작은	큰
jageun	*keun*

tight	bright
꼭 죄는	밝은
kkok joeneun	*balgeun*

(5) What a shopkeeper might say

Good morning sir.

안녕하세요?

annyeonghaseyo?

What do you want to buy?

무엇을 사려고 하십니까?
mu-eoseul saryeogo hasimnikka?

How many?

얼마나요?
eolmanayo?

What size?

크기는요?
keugineunyo?

What color do you want?

무슨 색상을 원하십니까?
museun saeksang-eul wonhasimnikka?

Do you want to try it on?

입어보고 싶습니까?
ibeobogo sipseumnikka?

Is this one all right?

이것이 맞는 것입니까?
igeosi manneun geosimnikka?

I will show you another.

다른 것을 보여드리겠습니다.
*dareun geoseul
boyeodeurigetseumnida.*

Do you want anything else?

이외에도 다른 것을 또 원하십니까?
*ioe-edo dareun geoseul tto
wonhasimnikka?*

Will you take it with you?

가져가시겠습니까?
gajeogasigetseumnikka?

We will send it to your hotel.

호텔까지 보내 드리겠습니다.
hotelkkaji bonae deurigetseumnida.

Shall we ship it to your home?

선편으로 보내 드릴까요?
seonpyeoneuro bonae deurilkkayo?

Please write down your address.

주소 좀 적어주십시오.
juso jom jeogeo jusipsio.

We don't have any <u>large</u>.

저희는 <u>큰 것이</u> 없습니다.

jeohuineun <u>keun geosi</u> eopseumnida.

Here is your bill.

여기 청구서가 있습니다.

yeogi cheongguseoga itseumnida.

Here is your change.

여기 거스름돈이 있습니다.

yeogi geoseureumdoni itseumnida.

This is your receipt.

여기 영수증이 있습니다.

yeogi yeongsujeung-i itseumnida.

Please come again.

또 오십시오.

tto osipsio.

6. Sightseeing

Sightseeing will naturally be one of your major activities in Korea and it will be a great reward to you. Where you go will depend on your particular personal interests. If you join a tour, choose one that visits the areas you want to see.

Local buses are overcrowded throughout downtown Seoul. However, they run very quickly and efficiently and are very convenient for traveling anywhere in the city. The bus fare is 1,000 won.

Express buses running on major highways are very convenient and efficient in traveling between major cities.

(1) About the weather

What is the weather like?

날씨가 어떻습니까?

nalssiga eotteoseumnikka?

It is beautiful.

> 화창합니다.
>
> *hwachanghamnida.*

It is hot.

> 덥습니다.
>
> *deopseumnida.*

It is very hot.

> 매우 덥습니다.
>
> *mae-u deopseumnida.*

It is sunny.

> 맑습니다.
>
> *makseumnida.*

It is bad.

> 좋지 않습니다.
>
> *jochi anseumnida.*

It is cool.

> 시원합니다.
>
> *siwonhamnida.*

It is cold.

춥습니다.

chupseumnida.

It is very cold.

매우 춥습니다.

mae-u chupseumnida.

It is windy.

바람이 붑니다.

barami bumnida.

It is foggy.

안개 끼었습니다.

angae kkieotseumnida.

It is raining.

비 옵니다.

bi omnida.

Is it going to rain today?

오늘 비 올까요?

oneul bi olkkayo?

It's too hot to go out.

외출하기에는 너무 덥습니다.

oechulhagieneun neomu deopseumnida.

(2) Visiting various places

Never fail to visit the museums. They are the places where the best things you have to see in the country are preserved. If you are on a tight schedule, don't spend too much of your time on window shopping, browsing around the stores, or on shopping. For those who remain home, a small, inexpensive souvenir, which is also light to carry, will do.

Mingle with the people of the country and get acquainted. Don't always stay in your own group. Have curiosity, and try to understand the people. Read the local newspapers, listen to the radio, and watch television and you will get much information.

I would like to go to see <u>an exhibition</u>.

나는 <u>전람회</u> 보러 가고 싶습니다.

naneun <u>jeollamhoe</u> boreo gago sipseumnida.

I would like to go to sightseeing.

나는 관광하고 싶습니다.

naneun gwan-gwanghago sipseumnida.

What are we going to see?

우리는 무엇을 보러 갑니까?

urineun mu-eoseul boreo gamnikka?

We are going to see <u>a ceramics</u>.

우리는 <u>도자기</u>보러 갑니다.

urineun <u>dojagi</u> boreo gamnida.

How long will the tour last?

여행은 얼마나 계속합니까?

yeohaeng-eun eolmana gyesokamnikka?

one hour	two hours
한 시간	두 시간
han sigan	*du sigan*

Are you our guide?

당신이 안내자입니까?

dangsini annaeja-imnikka?

No, the man over there is our guide.

아니요, 저기 있는 사람이 우리의 안내자입
니다.

*aniyo, jeogi inneun sarami uriui
annaeja-imnida.*

May I ask his name?

그분의 성함이 무엇입니까?

*geubunui seonghami
mu-eosimnikka?*

He is called Kim Myeong Su.

그의 성함은 김명수입니다.

*geuui seonghameun
kim myeongsu-imnida.*

Do you speak English?

영어를 말하십니까?

yeong-eoreul malhasimnikka?

I only speak a few words of English.

나는 영어를 조금밖에 못합니다.

*naneun yeong-eoreul
jogeumbakke motamnida.*

What time will the tour start?

몇 시에 여행이 시작됩니까?

*myeot sie yeohaeng-i
sijakdoemnikka?*

We'll leave the hotel at nine A.M.

아침 9시에 호텔을 출발합니다.

*achim ahopsie hotereul
chulbalhamnida.*

What time will we return?

몇 시에 돌아옵니까?

myeot sie doraomnikka?

We'll return at 3 P.M.

3시에 돌아옵니다.

sesie doraomnida.

Can we eat there?

> 거기서 식사할 수 있습니까?
> *geogiseo siksahal su itseumnikka?*

Of course, we can eat there.

> 물론 거기서 식사할 수 있습니다.
> *mullon geogiseo siksahal su itseumnida.*

Do we need tickets?

> 표가 있어야 합니까?
> *pyoga isseoya hamnikka?*

No, it's free.

> 아니요, 무료입니다.
> *aniyo, muryoimnida.*

Where do we meet?

> 어디서 만납니까?
> *eodiseo mannamnikka?*

In front of the hotel.

> 호텔 앞에서요.
> *hoterapeseoyo.*

How are we going to get there?

거기에 어떻게 갑니까?

geogie eotteoke gamnikka?

We are going by bus.

버스로 갑니다.

beoseuro gamnida.

(3) At the Site

What is the name of this place?

이곳은 이름이 무엇입니까?

igoseun ireumi mu-eosimnikka?

It's called <u>temple</u>.

이곳은 <u>절</u> 이라고 합니다.

igoseun <u>jeol</u> irago hamnida.

When was this place built?

이곳은 언제 지어졌습니까?

igoseun eonje jieojeotseumnikka?

It was built one hundred years ago.

이곳은 100년 전에 지어졌습니다.
*igoseun baeknyeon jeone jieo
jeotseumnida.*

May we go in?

들어가도 됩니까?
deureogado doemnikka?

Of course, you may.

물론 들어가도 됩니다.
mullon deureogado doemnida.

What is that place over there?

저 너머는 이름이 무엇입니까?
*jeo neomeoneun ireumi
mu-eosimnikka?*

May we take pictures?

사진을 찍어도 되나요?
sajineul jjigeodo doenayo?

Will you please take my picture?

제 사진을 찍으시겠습니까?
je sajineul jjigeusigetseumnikka?

What is this made of?

이것은 무엇으로 만들어졌나요?
*igeoseun mu-eoseuro
mandeureojeonnayo?*

It's made of <u>wood</u>.

이것은 <u>목재</u>로 만들어졌습니다.
*igeoseun <u>mokjae</u> ro
mandeureojeotseumnida.*

jade	bronze
구슬	청동
guseul	*cheongdon*
wood	copper
목재	구리
mokjae	*guri*

It's beautiful here.

이곳은 아름답습니다.
igoseun areumdapseumnida.

May we stay longer?

더 오래 머물 수 있나요?
deo orae meomul su innayo?

We must go back soon.

우리는 곧 돌아가야 합니다.

urineun got doragaya hamnida.

Can we buy a guide book?

안내 책자를 살 수 있습니까?

annae chaekjareul sal su itseumnikka?

Yes. It's very inexpensive.

네 그것은 매우 쌉니다.

ne geugeoseun mae-u ssamnida.

We would like to come again.

우리 다시 오고 싶습니다.

uri dasi ogo sipseumnida.

This place is <u>beautiful</u>.

이곳은 <u>아름다운</u> 곳입니다/습니다.

igoseun <u>areumdaun</u> gosimnida/seumnida.

beautiful	interesting
아름다운	재미있는
areumdaun	*jaemiinneun*

I am very tired.

> 나는 매우 피곤합니다.
> *naneun mae-u pigonhamnida.*

I want to rest for a few minutes.

> 나는 몇 분 동안 쉬고 싶습니다.
> *naneun myeot bun dong-an swigo sipseumnida.*

Is there a bathroom here?

> 여기 화장실이 있습니까?
> *yeogi hwajangsiri itseumnikka?*

Please tell me where it is.

> 그것이 어디 있는지 말씀해 주세요.
> *geugeosi eodi inneunji malsseumhae juseyo.*

I would like to have a drink of water.

> 물 한 잔 먹고 싶습니다.
> *mul han jan meokgo sipseumnida.*

Thank you very much.

> 매우 감사합니다.
> *mae-u gamsahamnida.*

I had a wonderful time today.

오늘 정말 즐거운 시간이었습니다.

oneul jeongmal jeulgeoun sigan ieotseumnida.

(4) Pursuing individual interests

We're interested in <u>sculpture</u>.

우리는 <u>조각</u>에 관심 있습니다.

urineun <u>jogak</u> e gwansim itseumnida.

antiques	sculpture
골동품	조각
goldongpum	*jogak*
archeology	fine arts
고고학	미술
gogohak	*misul*
art	furniture
예술	가구
yesul	*gagu*

ceramics, pottery	arts and crafts
도자기	미술 공예품
dojagi	*misul gong-yepum*
local crafts	Korean history
지방 토산물	한국사
jibang tosanmul	*han-guksa*
Korean painting	Korean music
한국화	한국음악
han-gukhwa	*han-gug eumak*

(5) Renting a car

There are a fair number of car rental services for visitors who wish to drive around the country. The rental fee ranges from about 50,000 won to 300,000 won per day. Even if you are a good driver, you should remember that driving in any downtown areas is not like driving in your native country. Streets are always crowded with cars, taxis, buses, and pedestrians. So be prepared.

A lot of taxis are moving in the major cities throughout downtown 24 hours. In Seoul and other cities you can rent a car easily. Taxis stop at designated taxi stands in front of department stores, hotels, railroad stations, and in certain areas downtown.

Taxis have the meter showing the fare in digits. There is an initial charge 1900 won for the first 2 kilometers and about 100 won for each additional 144 meters, about 100 won for each additional 35 seconds. In case of heavy traffic, taxis are moving slowly or halts. Even in such cases fare is added to the initial fare.

The call taxi can be called by telephone anywhere in downtown Seoul and hotel taxis are available at most major hotels. Some drivers speak English fairly well. If you encounter a taxidriver who does not speak English, ask someone ahead of time to write down your destination in Korean.

I would like to rent a car.

차를 빌리고 싶습니다.

chareul billigo sipseumnida.

How much will it cost to rent a car?

차 빌리는 데 얼마나 듭니까?

cha billineun de eolmana deumnikka?

Do they provide a driver?

운전사가 딸립니까?

unjeonsaga ttallimnikka?

Does the driver speak English?

운전사가 영어로 말할 수 있나요?

unjeonsaga yeong-eoro malhal su innayo?

(6) Where is the _____?

Where is the <u>palace</u>?

<u>궁전</u>은 어디에 있습니까?

<u>gungjeon</u> eun eodie itseumnikka?

palace	university
궁전	대학
gungjeon	*daehak*
statue	zoo
조각품	동물원
jogakpum	*dongmurwon*

are gallery	handicrafts shop
미술관	미술공예품
misulgwan	*misulgong-yepum*
theater	movie theater
극장	영화관
geukjang	*yeonghwagwan*
center of town	pagoda
도심지	탑
dosimji	*tap*
temple	park
절	공원
jeol	*gong-won*
pavilion	museum
정자	박물관
jeongja	*bangmulgwan*
garden	shopping district
화원	시장
hwawon	*sijang*

concert

음악회

eumakhoe

lake

호수

hosu

memorial hall

기념관

ginyeomgwan

memorial monument

기념비

ginyeombi

exhibition

전람회

jeollamhoe

opera house

오페라 극장

opera geukjang

(7) Is the _____ open today?

Is the <u>bookstore</u> open today?

> <u>서점</u>은 오늘 문을 열었습니까?
> <u>*seojeom*</u> *eun oneul muneul yeor-*
> *eotseumnikka?*

Yes, it's open today.

> 네, 오늘 문 열었습니다.
> *ne, oneul mun yeoreotseumnida.*

No, it's not open today.

> 아니요, 오늘 문 열지 않았습니다.
> *aniyo, oneul mun yeolji anatseumnida.*

It opens at nine a.m. and closes at five p.m.

> 거기는 오전 아홉 시에 열고 오후 다섯 시
> 에 닫습니다.
> *geogineun ojeon ahop sie yeolgo
> ohu daseot sie datseumnida.*

Is there an admission charge?

> 입장료가 있습니까?
> *ipjangnyoga itseumnikka?*

There's no charge.

> 입장료는 없습니다.
> *ipjangnyoneun eopseumnida.*

Is it far?

> 거리가 멉니까?
> *georiga meomnikka?*

Not at all. It's very close.

> 아니요, 매우 가깝습니다.
> *aniyo, mae-u gakkapseumnida.*

You can go by bus.

버스 타고 갈 수도 있습니다.
beoseu tago gal sudo itseumnida.

Please come with me.

나와 함께 갑시다.
nawa hamkke gapsida.

I would be happy to go with you.

당신과 함께 가게 되면 매우 기쁘겠습니다.
*dangsin-gwa hamkke gage
doemyeon maeu gippeugetseumnida.*

We have some free time tomorrow.

우리는 내일 여가가(시간이) 있습니다.
*urineun naeil yeogaga(sigani)
itseumnida.*

What shall we do for fun?

오락으로 무엇을 할까요?
orageuro mu-eoseul halkkayo?

I would like to <u>go to the park</u>.

나는 <u>공원에</u> 가고 싶습니다.
naneun <u>gong-wone</u> e gago sipseumnida.

see a play

연극 구경하다

yeon-geuk gugyeonghada

go to the botanical gardens

식물원에 가다.

singmurwone gada.

go to the park

공원에 가다

gong-wone gada

go hear a concert

음악회에 가다

eumakhoie gada

visit a ward(county) office

구(군)청에 가다

gu(gun)cheong-e gada

go to the zoo

동물원에 가다

dongmurwone gada

visit a factory

공장에 가다

gongjange gada

I don't want to go anywhere.

아무 곳에도 가고 싶지 않습니다.

amu gosedo gago sipji anseumnida.

I'm too tired.

나는 너무나 지쳤습니다.

naneun neomuna jicheotseumnida.

I want to relax.

나는 쉬고 싶습니다.

naneun swigo sipseumnida.

(8) Useful Signs

Entrance	Exit
입구	출구
ipgu	*chulgu*

East exit	West exit
동쪽 출구	서쪽 출구
dongjjok chulgu	*seojjok chulgu*
South exit	Keep out
남쪽 출구	출입 금지
namjjok chulgu	*churip geumji*
Danger	Under construction
위험	공사 중
wiheom	*gongsa jung*
Fire extinguisher	Lavotory
소화기	공중 화장실
sohwagi	*gongjung hwajangsil*
Elevator	Free required
승강기	유료
seungganggi	*yuryo*
Men	Women
신사	숙녀
sinsa	*sungnyeo*

Adult

성인

seong-in

Child

어린이

eorini

Business hours

영업시간

yeong-eop sigan

Closed hours

금일 휴업

geumil hyu-eop

Temporarily

임시 휴업

imsi hyu-eop

Staying open

야간 영업

yagan yeong-eop

No smoking

금연

geumyeon

Caution

주의

ju-ui

Parking place

주차장

juchajang

No parking

주차 금지

jucha geumji

Emergency

비상구

bisanggu

Don't touch

손대지 마시오

sondaeji masio

Waiting room	Information
대기실	안내소
daegisil	*annaeso*
Hospital	Please ring
병원	벨을 누르시오
byeong-weon	*bereul nureusio*
Pull	Push
당기시오	미시오
danggisio	*misio*
Beware of dog	Beware of fire
개주의	불조심
gaeju-ui	*buljosim*
Cashier	For rent
계산대	세 놓음
gyesandae	*se noeum*
No entry	No admittance
입장금지	입장금지
ipjang geumji	*ipjang geumji*

Private

개인용

gaeinyong

Private property

사유지

sayuji

Open

열었음

yeoreosseum

Closed

닫았음

dadasseum

For sale

매품

maepum

Sold out

매진

maejin

Stop

중지

jungji

Warning

경고

gyeonggo

Out of order

고장

gojang

Don't drink the water

마시지 못함

masiji motam

Not in use

사용금지

sayong geumji

Shoes off

신을 벗으시오

sineul beoseusio

Fit for drinking

음료수

eumnyosu

Now in session

회의 중

hoeui jung

Keep off the grass

잔디에 들어가지 마시오.

jandie deureogaji masio.

(9) Visiting a family

Allow plenty of time to get to your destination because traffic is usually heavy since you are a stranger here. Don't wait for the last moment and then rush to your appointment.

Bring a small gift for the hostess when you are invited. Don't arrive empty-handed. When you are invited to a formal dinner, don't forget to take your invitation with you. You may have to present it when you arrive.

When arriving at any formal event, don't carry your coat into the main reception area. Check it with the cloakroom attendants. Wait till you've greeted the host and the guest of honor before having a drink.

When meeting people, Koreans usually exchange their

calling cards after a firm handshake. Give your card only after you are introduced. But when you visit an office, give your card to the secretary or receptionist right away. Be careful not to sit just anywhere you want to, but wait to be offered a chair.

Here are some suggestions to make your visit more pleasant: Good manners, patience, and courtesy are always in order. Be on time for all activities.

I would like to invite you to dinner.

> 선생님을 저녁식사에 초대하고 싶습니다.
> *seonsaengnimeul jeonyeoksiksa−e chodaehago sipseumnida.*

I'm very happy (to come). Thank you.

> 매우 기쁩니다. 감사합니다.
> *mae−u gippeumnida. gamsahamnida.*

What time shall we go?

> 몇 시에 가나요?
> *myeot sie ganayo?*

We'll go at 7:30.

> 일곱시 삼십분에 갈 겁니다.
> *ilgopsi samsipbune gal geomnida.*

Where shall we meet?

우리 어디에서 만날까요?

uri eodieseo mannalkkayo?

In front of the hotel.

호텔 앞에서 (만납시다)

hoterapeseo (mannapsida)

May I bring a friend?

친구를 데려갈까요?

chin-gureul deryeogalkkayo?

Of course, you may.

물론 좋습니다.

mullon joseumnida.

Where shall we eat?

어디서 식사할까요?

eodiseo siksahalkkayo?

Let's eat at a Lotte Hotel restaurant.

롯데호텔 식당에서 식사합시다.

rotdehotel sikdang-eseo siksahapsida.

(10) Adminstrative Divisions and Geographic Regions

city

시

si

district

구

gu

dong (subdistrict)

동

dong

province

도

do

gun

군

gun

myeon

면

myeon

ri

리

ri

region, area

지역/지방

jiyeok/jibang

Gyeonggi Province

경기도

gyeonggi-do

Gangwon Province

강원도

gangwon-do

S(N). Chungcheong Province

충청남도(충청북도)

chungcheong nam-do(buk-do)

S(N). Jeolla Province

전라남도(전라북도)

jeolla nam-do(buk-do)

S(N). Gyeongsang Province

경상남도(경상북도)

gyeongsang nam-do(buk-do)

Jeju Province

제주도

jeju-do

Gyeonggi Region

경기 지역

gyeonggi jiyeok

Gangwon Region

강원 지역

gangwon jiyeok

Chungcheong Region

충청 지역

chungcheong jiyeok

Honam Region

호남 지역

honam jiyeok

Jeju Region

제주 지역

jeju jiyeok

7. Traveling

Most international flights to Korea arrive at Incheon International Airport which is about 70 minutes by bus from the center of Seoul. Information on transportation or sightseeing are available at the airport information desk.

Tour groups within a city will often travel by tour buses, which are mostly comfortable and air-conditioned. Individual by the regular local bus is inexpensive and will give you a chance to use the phrases you've learned so far. If you plan to travel alone, it's a good idea to check with your guide first. Work out the details of your trip with him or her.

Taxis are available for both business and sightseeing, but they're quite expensive. You can arrange for a taxi with the help of your hotel service desk.

(1) By Airplane

I want to go to <u>Busan</u> by plane.

저는 비행기로 <u>부산</u>에 가고 싶습니다.

jeoneun bihaenggiro <u>busan</u> e gago sipseumnida.

Busan	Daegu
부산	대구
busan	*daegu*

Jeju-do	Ulsan
제주도	울산
jeju-do	*ulsan*

Gwangju	Gyeongju
광주	경주
gwangju	*gyeongju*

Is there a plane to <u>Hawaii</u>?

하와이에 가는 비행기가 있습니까?
<u>hawaii</u> e ganeun bihaenggiga itseumnikka?

Hongkong	Philippine
홍콩	필리핀
hongkong	*pillipin*

Hawaii	Guam
하와이	괌
hawa-i	*gwam*

Australia

호주

hoju

When does the plane take off?

비행기가 언제 출발합니까?

bihaenggiga eonje chulbalhamnikka?

Where can I buy a plane ticket?

비행기표를 어디서 살 수 있습니까?

bihaenggipyoreul eodiseo sal su itseumnikka?

I want to buy two tickets to Busan.

저는 부산행 표 두 장을 사고 싶습니다.

jeoneun busanhaeng pyo du jang-eul sago sipseumnida.

How much is the ticket price?

표 값이 얼마입니까?

pyo gapsi eolma-imnikka?

Do you want a one-way ticket or a round-trip ticket?

편도표를 드릴까요, 왕복표를 드릴까요?
*pyeondopyoreul deurilkkayo
wangbokpyoreul deurilkkayo?*

One way ticket.

편도표입니다.
pyeondopyo-imnida.

Round-trip ticket.

왕복표입니다.
wangbokpyo-imnida.

What time should I go to the airport?

공항에 몇 시에 가야 합니까?
*gonghang-e myeot sie gaya
hamnikka?*

Before two thirty.

두시 삼십분 전에요.
dusi samsipbun jeoneyo.

What is the flight number?

비행기는 몇 번입니까?
bihaenggineun myeot beonimnikka?

Flight 262.

이륙이번입니다.

iryug-ibeonimnida.

What time do we arrive?

몇 시에 도착합니까?

myeot sie dochakamnikka?

We arrive at 6 p.m.

여섯시에 도착합니다.

yeoseotsie dochakamnida.

Are you the stewardess?

당신이 스튜어디스입니까?

dangsini seutyu-eodiseu-imnikka?

Please help me with my bags.

가방을 좀 들어주십시오.

gabang-eul jom deureojusipsio.

Please help me.

도와주십시오.

dowajusipsio.

I don't feel well.

몸이 좋지 않습니다.

momi jochi anseumnida.

I'm hungry.

저는 배가 좀 고픕니다.

jeoneun baega jom gopeumnida.

Is there anything to eat?

먹을 것이 있나요?

meogeul geosi innayo?

I'm thirsty.

저는 목이 마릅니다.

jeoneun mogi mareumnida.

I'd like some water.

물 좀 마시고 싶습니다.

mul jom masigo sipseumnida.

Where's the toilet?

화장실은 어디에 있습니까?

hwajangsireun eodie itseumnikka?

It's in the rear.

뒤에 있습니다.

dwie itseumnida.

*Flying Times Between Major Cities

Seoul-Jeju	서울-제주	65 minutes
Seoul-Busan	서울-부산	60 minutes
Seoul-Daegu	서울-대구	50 minutes
Seoul-Gwangju	서울-광주	50 minutes
Seoul-Ulsan	서울-울산	55 minutes

(2) By Train

Traveling by train in Korea is very convenient and efficient. The railroad system operated by the KORAIL(Korea Rail Road) has extensive connections from Seoul to most large cities.

Three types of trains can be employed for traveling as follows:

KTX	Saemaeul Express
케이티엑스	새마을호
keitiekseu	*saema-eulho*

Mugunghwa Express

무궁화호
mugunghwaho

I want to reserve <u>KTX</u>.

<u>케이티엑스</u>를 예약하고 싶습니다.
<u>keitiekseu</u> reul yeyakago sipseumnida.

Is the train station far from here?

여기서 기차역이 멉니까?
yeogiseo gichayeogi meomnikka?

It will only take a few minutes to get there.

거기까지 불과 몇 분 안 걸립니다.
geogikkaji bulgwa myeot bun an geollimnida.

Where's the ticket office?

매표소는 어디에 있습니까?
maepyosoneun eodie itseumnikka?

It's over there.

저기에 있습니다.
jeogie itseumnida.

Is there a train for <u>Busan</u>?

부산가는 기차 있습니까?

<u>busan</u> *ganeun gicha itseumnikka?*

Yes. / No.

네/아니요.

ne/aniyo.

Please give me a time-table in English.

영어로 된 시간표 좀 주세요.

yeong-eoro doen siganpyo jom juseyo.

I want to buy a ticket to Busan.

부산행 표를 사고 싶습니다.

Busanhaeng pyoreul sago sipseumnida.

How much is the fare?

요금은 얼마입니까?

yogeumeun eolma-imnikka?

Forty-eight thousand won.

48,000원입니다.

saman palcheon wonimnida.

At 4:00 p.m.

4시에 출발합니다.

nesie chulbalhamnida.

Better hurry.

서두르는 게 좋겠어요.

seodureuneun ge jokesseoyo.

The train will leave shortly!

기차가 바로 출발합니다!

gichaga baro chulbalhamnida!

Which track/platform?

몇 번 선로에서요?

myeot beon seollo-eseoyo?

Number five.

오번입니다.

obeonimnida.

When is the next train?

다음 기차는 언제 있습니까?

daeum gichaneun eonje itseumnikka?

Please help me with my luggage.

짐을 나르는데 도와주십시오.

jimeul nareuneunde dowajusipsio.

All aboard!

모두 타세요!

modu taseyo!

(3) By Car

Can I take a trip to Busan by car?

부산까지 차로 갈 수 있습니까?

busankkaji charo gal su itseumnikka?

That is very long trip.

매우 먼 여행입니다.

mae-u meon yeohaeng-imnida.

How long will it take me?

제게는 얼마나 걸릴까요?

jegeneun eolmana geollilkkayo?

About six hours.

약 6시간요.

yak yeoseot siganyo.

What can I see there?

거기서 무엇을 볼 수 있나요?

geogiseo mu-eoseul bol su innayo?

Are there many routes to take?

교통편이 거기에 많습니까?

gyotongpyeoni geogie manseumnikka?

Can I see one of the national parks on the way?

가는 도중에 국립공원 하나를 볼 수 있나요?

ganeun dojung-e gungnipgong-won hanareul bol su innayo?

Is Gyeongju a wonderful city?

경주는 아름다운 도시인가요?

gyeongjuneun areumdaun dosi ingayo?

It seems that Gyeongju has everything.

경주에는 모든 게 다 있는 것 같아요.

gyeongju-eneun modeun ge da inneun geot gatayo.

There is no place exactly like Gyeongju in Korea.

한국에는 경주 만한 곳이 없습니다.

han-gugeneun gyeongju manhan gosi eopseumnida.

*Terms of Travel and Transportation

travel(ler)	tour(ist)
여행(자)	관광(객)
yeohaeng(ja)	*gwan-gwang(gaek)*
airplane	airport
비행기	공항
bihaenggi	*gonghang*
international airport	jet plane
국제공항	제트기
gukjegonghang	*jeteugi*

international line	domestic (air)line
국제선	국내선
gukjeseon	*gungnaeseon*
travel agency	customs
여행사	세관
yeohaengsa	*se-gwan*
reservation	tax
예약	세금
yeyak	*segeum*
passport	luggage, suitcase
여권	가방
yeo-gwon	*gabang*
visa	baggage, load
비자	짐
bija	*jim*
carry-on luggage	ship, boat
휴대품	선박, 배
hyudaepum	*seonbak, bae*

train	subway
기차, 열차	지하철
gicha, yeolcha	*jihacheol*
freight, cargo	passenger boat
화물	여객선
hwamul	*yeogaekseon*
cargo ship	freight car(train)
화물선	화물열차
hwamulseon	*hwamul yeolcha*
bus	express bus
버스	고속버스
beoseu	*gosokbeoseu*
express(high) way	taxi
고속도로	택시
gosokdoro	*taeksi*
car	fare
차/자동차	요금
cha/jadongcha	*yogeum*

truck

트럭

teureok

rest area

휴식처

hyusikcheo

restroom

화장실

hwajangsil

shop, store

상점

sangjeom

January 1
New Year's day

양력 설날

yangnyeok seolnal

1st day of lunar January
Folklore Day

음력 설날

eumnyeok seolnal

March 1
Independence Movement Day

삼일절

samil jeol

April 5
Labor Day

식목일

singmogil

May 5
Children's Day

어린이날

eorininal

8th day of 4th
Buddha's Birthday

석가탄신일

seokga tansinil

July 17
Constitution Day

제헌절

jeheonjeol

June 6
Memorial Day

현충일

hyeonchung-il

August 15
Liberation Day

광복절

gwangbokjeol

15th day of 8th(lunar)
Chuseok

추석

chuseok

October 3
National Foundation Day

개천절

gaecheonjeol

October 9
Korean Alphabet Day

한글날

han-geulnal

December 25(Christmas)

성탄절

seongtanjeol

Seoul	서울	Pyeongtaek	평택
Incheon	인천	Daegu	대구
Anyang	안양	Busan	부산
Suwon	수원	Ulsan	울산
Masan	마산	Daejeon	대전
Mokpo	목포	Onyang	온양
Gwangju	광주	Chuncheon	춘천
Jeonju	전주	Cheongju	청주
Wonju	원주	Gangneung	강릉
Sokcho	속초		

8.Relaxing

Korea offers you many places where you can sit back and enjoy. Korea is a land of contrasts with many ways to relax and many forms of entertainment from nong-ak(a kind of farmers' music) performances to dynamic talchum(a kind of traditional dance).

There are plays, movies, sports, restaurants with live stage performances, night clubs and so forth. Enjoy the spectacle and the people.

(1) Useful Expressions

Where shall we go tonight?

오늘 저녁 어디 갈까요?

oneul jeonyeok eodi galkkayo?

I want to go and <u>see the ballet</u>.

저는 <u>발레</u>보러 가고 싶습니다.

jeoneun <u>balle</u> boreo gago sipseumnida.

see the ballet

발레 보러

balle boreo

see the movie

영화 보러

yeonghwa boreo

hear a concert

연주 들으러

yeonju deureureo

see the opera

오페라 브러

opera boreo

see a Korean movie

한국영화 보러

han-gug-yeonghwa boreo

see a foreign movie

외국영화 보러

oegug-yeonghwa boreo

go to a bar

술집에

suljibe

go to a nightclub

나이트클럽에

naiteukeulleobe

go to a restaurant

식당에

sikdang-e

see the circus

서커스 보러

seokeoseu boreo

see a sporting event

스포츠 경기 보러

spocheu gyeonggi boreo

How should I dress?

어떻게 옷을 입을까요?

eotteoke oseul ibeulkkayo?

Any sort of clothes will do.

어떤 옷도 괜찮습니다.

eotteon otdo gwaenchanseumnida.

What movie is showing today?

오늘 어떤 영화가 상연되나요?

oneul eotteon yeonghwaga sang-yeondoenayo?

What time does it start?

몇 시에 시작하나요?

myeot sie sijakanayo?

What time does it end?

몇 시에 끝나나요?

myeot sie kkeunnanayo?

Do we need tickets?

표를 사야 되나요?
pyoreul saya doenayo?

Please call a taxi.

택시 좀 불러주십시오.
taeksi jom bulleojusipsio.

I want to go to <u>a bar</u>.

저는 <u>술집</u>에 가고 싶습니다.
jeoneun <u>suljib</u> e gago sipseumnida.

Good evening, My name is <u>huisu</u>.

안녕하세요, 저는 <u>희수</u>입니다.
annyeonghaseyo, jeoneun <u>huisu</u> imnida.

I have already reserved a table.

제가 벌써 테이블을 예약했습니다.
jega beolsseo teibeureul yeyakaetseumnida.

Is food served here?

음식이 여기서 제공되나요?
eumsigi yeogiseo jegongdoenayo?

Can we buy a drinks?

음료도 살 수 있나요?

eumnyodo sal su innayo?

How do you do.

처음 뵙겠습니다.

cheo-eum boepgetseumnida.

How are you!

안녕하세요?

annyeonghaseyo?

My name is <u>suil</u>.

제 이름은 <u>수일</u>입니다.

je ireumeun <u>suil</u> imnida.

I'm an American.

저는 미국인입니다.

jeoneun miguginimnida.

I'm a foreigner.

저는 외국인입니다.
jeoneun oeguginimnida.

What's your name?

당신의 이름은 무엇입니까?
dangsinui ireumeun mu-eosimnikka?

May I introduce <u>Mr. Kim</u>?

<u>김씨</u>를 소개할까요?
<u>kim ssi</u> reul sogaehalkkayo?

I would like to meet a friend of mine.

제 친구를 만나보셨으면 좋겠습니다.
je chin-gureul mannabosyeosseu-myeon joketseumnida.

This is <u>my wife</u>.

이 사람은 <u>나의 아내</u>입니다.
i sarameun <u>naui anae</u> imnida.

How long have you been in Korea?

한국에 얼마나 계셨습니까?
han-guge eolmana gyesyeotseumnikka?

I've been here about two weeks.

약 2주쯤 있었습니다.
yak ijujjeum isseotseumnida.

Are you enjoying yourself?

재미있는 시간을 보내고 있습니까?
jaemiinneun siganeul bonaego itseumnikka?

We're very busy.

우리는 매우 바쁩니다.
urineun mae-u bappeumnida.

Did you come alone?

혼자 오셨습니까?
honja osyeotseumnikka?

my wife

나의 아내
naui anae

my family

나의 가족
naui gajok

my parents

나의 부모
naui bumo

9.Communicating

Everywhere you will see payphone booths where you can either use coins (10, 50, 100 denominations) or your plastic card. From a public booth you may call overseas, see your hotel clerk or ask a friend since rates for such are rather high.

Local calls cost 70 won, is very cheap when compared with other countries. Long-distance calls also possible by public telephone calls if you have a plastic phone card.

If you plan to call home, remember that Korean time is different.

(1)Making a call

Is there a telephone here?

여기 전화기 있습니까?

yeogi jeonhwagi itseumnikka?

May I use the phone?

전화 좀 써도 됩니까?

jeonhwa jom sseodo doemnikka?

Please help me make a telephone call.

전화 거는 데 좀 도와주세요.
jeonhwa geoneun de jom dowajuseyo.

I want to make a phone call to <u>my wife</u>.

<u>나의 아내</u>에게 전화하고 싶습니다.
<u>*naui anae*</u> *ege jeonhwahago sipseumnida.*

My friend, Mr. Smith

나의 친구 스미스씨

naui chin-gu seumiseussi

a Korean restaurant

한국 식당

han-guk sikdang

the American Embassy   the hotel

미국대사관   호텔

migug daesagwan   hotel

How do I make a long distance call?

장거리 전화를 어떻게 합니까?
janggeori jeonhwareul eotteoke hamnikka?

Please go to the service desk to handle it.

담당 안내역한테로 가세요.

damdang annaeyeoghantero gaseyo.

(2) In the street

Can you speak English?

영어를 하십니까?
yeong-eoreul hasimnikka?

What?

뭐라고요?
mworagoyo?

I know very little English.

영어를 조금 압니다.
yeong-eoreul jogeum amnida.

What did you say?

뭐라고 말씀하셨습니까?
mworago malsseumhasyeot-seumnikka?

Is there anyone who speaks English?

영어를 말하는 사람 있습니까?

yeong-eoreul malhaneun saram itseumnikka?

Speak slowly, please.

좀 천천히 말씀해 주십시오.

jom cheoncheonhi malsseumhae jusipsio.

Do you understand?

아시겠습니까?

asigetseumnikka?

No, I don't understand.

아니요, 모르겠습니다.

aniyo, moreugetseumnida.

Excuse me, could you help me.

실례합니다. 저 좀 도와주시겠습니까?

sillyehamnida. jeo jom dowajusigetseumnikka?

Please say it again.

> 다시 좀 말씀해 주십시오.
> *dasi jom malsseumhae jusipsio.*

Who is that?

> 저분은 누구십니까?
> *jeobuneun nugusimnikka?*

Pardon me, may I introduce myself?

> 실례지만 저를 소개해도 되겠습니까?
> *sillyejiman jeoreul sogaehaedo*
> *doegetseumnikka?*

How do you do?

> 처음 뵙겠습니다.
> *cheo-eum boepgetseumnida.*

I'm glad to see you.

> 만나서 반갑습니다.
> *mannaseo bangapseumnida.*

I would like to meet him.

> 그분을 만나보고 싶습니다.
> *geubuneul mannabogo sipseumnida.*

My name is Michael.

저는 마이클입니다.
jeoneun maikeurimnida.

Would you introduce me to him?

저를 그분에게 소개해 주시겠습니까?
*jeoreul geubunege sogaehae
jusigetseumnikka?*

May I have your card?

선생님의 명함을 좀 주시겠습니까?
*seonsaengnimui myeonghameul jom
jusigetseumnikka?*

Here's my card.

제 명함입니다.
je myeonghamimnida.

Where are you from?

어디서 오셨습니까?
eodiseo osyeotseumnikka?

Are you from <u>Seoul</u>?

<u>서울</u>에서 오셨습니까?
<u>seoul</u> eseo osyeotseumnikka?

I'm from <u>Busan</u>.

저는 <u>부산</u>에서 왔습니다.
jeoneun <u>busan</u> eseo watseumnida.

How long will you be here?

얼마 동안 여기에 계시겠습니까?
eolma dong-an yeogie gyesigetseumnikka?

Where are you staying?

어디에 머물고 있습니까?
eodie meomulgo itseumnikka?

Where can I call you?

어디로 연락하면 됩니까?
eodiro yeollakamyeon doemnikka?

Here's my address and phone number.

제 주소와 전화번호입니다.
je jusowa jeonhwabeonho-imnida.

Thanks a lot.

대단히 고맙습니다.
daedanhi gomapseumnida.

Can you pick me up tomorrow morning?

내일 아침 저를 태워주실 수 있습니까?

naeil achim jeoreul taewojusil su itseumnikka?

See you tomorrow morning.

내일 아침에 봅시다.

naeil achime bopsida.

See you later.

나중에 만납시다.

najung-e mannapsida.

PART III
FOR
BUSINESS
TRAVELERS

1. Business Customs in Korea

Businessmen always try to seek our new markets for their products, to develop more efficient ways to distribute or sell their goods to more people. So they often travel to foreign countries where language and customs are different. Even when a businessman knows the Korean language, the specialized and often idiosyncratic terminology of the business world can be an obstacle to successful negotiations. Here is an essential pocket reference for all business travelers to Korea. Whether your business is manufacturing or finance, communications or sales, this part will put the right words in your mouth and the best possible expressions in your correspondence.

Korea also has its peculiarities with respect to customs and culture. Over the past centuries Confucianism has exerted a great deal of influence on Korean mores. In many instances, manners and life styles are quite different from those of Western countries, One may say that business is a matter of sentiment. That is why businessmen should understand the cultural background when doing business with Koreans. In this vein, the following points will prove useful to you as you try to develop a successful business transaction.

① Learn how to use chopsticks. Once accustomed to using them, you will find them coming handy both as a means of picking food and showing off your dexterity at handling an odd custom of your host or hostess.

② Should you want to conduct serious business negotiations, meet your counterpart in Persons. Like other people whose cultures are rooted in oral tradition, Koreans prefer to talk in person rather than by phone or written correspondence about matters that require sure comprehension and hard thinking.

③ When entering someone's home, be sure to take your shoes off. This unwritten rule should be observed especially when you enter a home with ondol floor. And this is a custom still in effect throughout the country. Remember the fact that Koreans as any other poeple want to keep their rcom always clean in any case.

④ Beware that Koreans in general do not like to make an eye-to-eye contact all the time when engaged in a conversation because to them it sometimes implies impoliteness or rudness.

⑤ Never write any personal names or even short memos in red ink because it is considered sinister. Red ink is used only when you stamp your tojang(the chop of seal) on documents.

⑥ Also beware that Koreans always say or write their surnames (or family names) first, then the given name followed by a suitable honorific title such as "seonsaeng-nim" (meaning "Mr" or "Sir") and other formal titles (see the common business terms, plus the "Cure-all" suffix indicating respect "nim").

⑦ For reasons of trust building, it is usually good idea

for you to be introduced to government officials or company representatives through a friend of yours or someone you already know.

⑧ A trip to a bar or a restaurant usually means an extension of business although at times the substance of your talk may not be explicitly related to business.

⑨ If you don't know how to behave in some cases, you can ask or use any good Western manners.

⑩ You don't need to show gratitude at hotel because all costs are already included in your bill.

⑪ Sometimes it is effective to be introduced to officials through your acquaintance in order to maintain a positive relationship with him.

⑫ If Koreans take you to a bar or restaurant, it is usually a part of business.

(1) Business Meeting

Hello, Good morning.

안녕하십니까?

annyeonghasimnikka?

How do you do?

처음 뵙겠습니다.
cheo-eum boepgetseumnida.

What's your name?

성함이 어떻게 되십니까?
seonghami eotteoke doesimnikka?

I am <u>suil</u>.

저는 <u>수일</u>입니다.
jeoneun <u>suil</u> imnida.

Do you speak English?

영어를 하십니까?
yeong-eoreul hasimnikka?

I speak a little Korean.

한국말을 조금 합니다.
han-gungmareul jogeum hamnida.

What did you say?

뭐라고 말씀하셨습니까?
*mworago malsseumhasyeot-
seumnikka?*

Please repeat it slowly.

다시 천천히 말씀해 주십시오.
dasi cheoncheonhi malsseumhae jusipsio.

Excuse me. What does this mean?

실례지만 이것이 무슨 뜻입니까?
sillyejiman igeosi museun tteusimnikka?

I don't understand.

저는 모르겠습니다.
jeoneun moreugetseumnida.

It doesn't matter.

_ 괜찮습니다.
gwaenchanseumnida.

_ 상관없습니다.
sanggwan eopseumnida.

Where are the restrooms?

화장실이 어디 있습니까?
hwajangsiri eodi itseumnikka?

Would you call me a cab, please?

대단히 좀 불러 주시겠습니까?

taeksi jom bulleo jusigetseumnikka?

Thank you very much.

대단히 감사합니다.

daedanhi gamsahamnida.

What time is it?

지금 몇 시입니까?

jigeum myeot siimnikka?

Good-bye.

안녕히 가십시오.
annyeonghi gasipsio.

(2) At the Lodging

Do you have any messages for me?

저한테 무슨 연락 온 것 있습니까?
*jeohante museun yeollag on geot
itseumnikka?*

Is the barber still open?

이발소가 아직도 열려 있습니까?
ibalsoga ajikdo yeollyeo itseumnikka?

Where can I buy English-language newspapers?

영자 신문을 어디서 살 수 있습니까?
yeongja sinmuneul eodiseo sal su itseumnikka?

(3) Looking for Help

I'm lost.

길을 잃었습니다.
gireul ireotseumnida.

Where is the post office?

우체국이 어디에 있습니까?
uchegugi eodie itseumnikka?

And the mailbox?

우체통은요?
uchetong-eunyo?

I would like to make a phone call.

전화 걸고 싶습니다.

jeonhwa geolgo sipseumnida.

2.Banking

Banking services are available in many places in Korea. Traveler's checks are accepted and can be converted easily. Double check with your travel agency to make sure your particular traveler's checks will be accepted. Carry your passport when you do your banking. Keep records of all your currency exchanges. Remember that you must declare your foreign currency.

The official name for Korean currency is won. The bank notes come in 100, 500, 1,000, 5,000 and 10,000 won denominations; coins in 10, 50, 100, and 500 won denominations.

The exchange rate is subject to change depending on the daily fluctuations of the foreign money market, although the won is closely tied to the U.S. dollar. The current exchange rate is about 940 won to the U.S. dollar, as of the early of August, 2007. Information about the current exchange rates is available at banks, tourist offices, and hotels.

(1) Basic Words

ten thousand won	five thousand won
만 원	오천 원
man won	*ocheon won*

one thousand won	five hundred won
천 원	오백 원
cheon won	*obaeg won*
one hundered won	one hundred dollars
백 원	백 달러
baeg won	*baek dalleo*
three dollars	forty cents
삼 달러	사십 센트
sam dalleo	*sasip senteu*
twenty five cents	five cents
이십오 센트	오 센트
isib osenteu	*o senteu*

(2) To the Bank

Where's the bank?

은행이 어디에 있습니까?

eunhaeng-i eodie itseumnikka?

The nearest is on <u>10 minutes</u> away.

가장 가까운 것은 <u>10분</u> 거리/로에 있습니다.
*gajang gakkaun geoseun sip-bun
geori/ro-e itseumnida.*

What time does it open?

몇 시에 문을 엽니까?
myeot sie muneul yeomnikka?

It opens at nine half.

9시 30분에 엽니다.
ahopsi samsipbune yeomnida.

It closes at four half.

4시 30분에 닫습니다.
nesi samsipbune datseumnida.

Does it open Saturday, also?

토요일에도 여나요?
toyoiredo yeonayo?

No, it doesn't.

아니오, 열지 않습니다.
anio, yeolji anseumnida.

Where can I exchange American dollars?

어디서 미국달러를 바꿀 수 있나요?

eodiseo miguk dalleoreul bakkul su innayo?

Where can I exchange Hong Kong dollars?

어디서 홍콩달러를 바꿀 수 있나요?

eodiseo hongkong dalleoreul bakkul su innayo?

Where can I exchange British pounds?

어디서 영국 돈을 바꿀 수 있나요?

eodiseo yeongguk doneul bakkul su innayo?

I want to cash a Traveler's Check.

여행자 수표를 바꾸고 싶습니다.

yeohaengja supyoreul bakkugo sipseumnida.

Go to that clerk, please.

저분한테 가세요.
jeobunhante gaseyo.

How much do you want to exchange?

얼마나 바꾸시겠어요?
eolmana bakkusigesseoyo?

Fifty dollars.

50달러요.
osipdalleoyo.

May I see your passport?

여권 좀 보여주시겠어요?
yeo-gwon jom boyeojusigesseoyo?

Here is my passport.

여기 제 여권이 있습니다.
yeogi je yeo-gwoni itseumnida.

Will you accept traveler's checks?

여행자 수표를 받으시겠어요?
*yeohaengja supyoreul
badeusigesseoyo?*

Yes (I/ we do).

네, 받습니다.
ne, batseumnida.

Can you cash a personal check?

자기앞 수표도 바꾸어 주나요?
jagiap supyodo bakkueo junayo?

Do you have any personal I.D.?

신분증을 가지고 계세요?
sinbunjeung-eul gajigo gyeseyo?

Yes, I have a passport.

네, 여권이 있습니다.
ne, yeo-gwoni itseumnida.

Please sign here.

여기 사인 좀 해주세요.
yeogi sain jom haejuseyo.

Who speaks English here?

여기서 누가 영어를 말합니까?
yeogiseo nuga yeong-eoreul malhamnikka?

I have a letter of introduction.

저는 소개장이 있습니다.

jeoneun sogaejang-i itseumnida.

Please give me 100 dollars in Korean currency.

100달러 좀 원화로 바꾸어 주세요.

baekdalleo jom wonhwaro bakkueo juseyo.

Please count it to see if it is correct.

맞는지 세어 보세요.

manneunji seeo boseyo.

Will you please sign this receipt?

이 영수증에 사인 좀 해주세요.

i yeongsujeung-e sain jom haejuseyo.

Here's your change.

여기 거스름돈이 있습니다.

yeogi geoseureumdoni itseumnida.

I want to open a bank account.

은행구좌를 트고 싶습니다.

eunhaenggujwareul teugo sipseumnida.

I would like to deposit some money.

돈을 좀 예금하고 싶습니다.

doneul jom yegeumhago sipseumnida.

Which form do I use?

어떤 용지에 써야 하나요?

eotteon yongjie sseoya hanayo?

Where do I sign?

어디에 사인해야 되나요?

eodie sainhaeya doenayo?

What is the exchange rate today?

오늘 환율은 얼마인가요?

oneul hwanyureun eolma-ingayo?

Bank of Korea

한국은행

han-guk-eunhaeng

Foreign Exchange Bank

외환은행

oehwan-eunhaeng

City Bank

시티은행

siti-eunhaeng

Industrial Bank of Korea

기업은행

gieop-eunhaeng

Kookmin Bank

국민은행

Kookmin-eunhaeng

Woori Bank

우리은행

uri-eunhaeng

Chief of Branch

지점장

jijeomjang

President of Bank

은행장

eunhaengjang

branch

지점

jijeom

check

수표

supyo

insurance	personal check
보험	자기앞 수표
boheom	*jagiap supyo*
window	deposit
창구	예금
changgu	*yegeum*
withdraw	cash
대출	현금
daechul	*hyeon-geum*
insurance company	contract(document)
보험회사	계약(서)
boheomhoesa	*gyeyak(seo)*
sales contract	ownership, title
판매계약	소유권
panmaegyeyak	*soyu-gwon*
sales dept.	advertising dept.
판매부	광고부
panmaebu	*gwanggobu*

business dept.

사업부

sa-eopbu

(5) Titles of Businessmen/women

chairman

회장

hoejang

president

사장

sajang

vice president

부사장

busajang

executive director

전무

jeonmu

director

상무

sangmu

division chief

부장

bujang

bureau chief

국장

gukjang

deputy chief

차장

chajang

head of department	section
과장	실장
gwajang	*siljang*
assistant head	unit leader
대리	계장
daeri	*gyejang*
board member	board of directors
이사	이사진*
isa	*isajin*
board chairman	
이사장	
isajang	

Note that all these titles except the one marked are usually followed by the honorific affix "nim" especially in a face-to-face situation where a measure of formality is necessary.

abstract of title

권리증서

gwollijeungseo

account

구좌

gujwa

account balance

구좌 잔고

gujwa jan-go

account period

거래 기간

georae gigan

adjusted CIF price

운임-보험료 포함 조정 가격

unim-boheomnyo poham jojeong gagyeok

advance notice

사전 통고

sajeon tonggo

advertising agency

광고대행업

gwanggo daehaeng-eop

afterdate

후불하다

hubulhada

agency

대리점

daerijeom

aggregate demand

총수요
chongsuyo

arbitrage

중개 거래
junggae georae

at par

액면 그대로
aengmyeon geudaero

at the opening

개장 시
gaejang si

authorized dealer

공인중개사
gong-in junggaesa

back date

연체일
yeoncheil

approved securities

공인유가증권
gong-in yuga jeunggwon

associate company

동업자 회사
dong-eopja hoesa

at the market

시장 가격으로
sijang gagyeogeuro

attestation

증명서
jeungmyeongseo

average price

평균가격
pyeonggyun gagyeok

balance of payments

국제수지
gukje suji

balance of trade

무역수지
muyeok suji

balance

은행잔고
eunhaeng jan-go

bank deposit

은행예금
eunhaeng yegeum

bankruptcy

파산
pasan

barter

물물교환하다
mulmul gyohwan hada

below par

액면이하로
aengmyeon iharo

bid

입찰
ipchal

blue chip stock

우량주식
uryang jusik

business management

사업경영
sa-eop gyeong-yeong

bill of exchange

환어음
hwan eoeum

capital market

자본시장
jabon sijang

cable transfer

전신환
jeonsinhwan

capital, working

운영자본
unyeong jabon

capital surplus

자본잉여금
jabon ing-yeogeum

cash delivery

현금인도
hyeon-geum indo

carnet

무관세 허가증
mu-gwanse heogajeung

cash in advance

선불
seonbul

cashier's check

자기앞 수표
jagiap supyo

ceiling

상한선
sanghanseon

certified public accountant

공인회계사
kong-in hoegyesa

charge account

외상거래 계정
oesanggeorae gyejeong

chief executive

최고 경영인
choego gyeong-yeong-in

checklist

대조표
daejopyo

classified ad.

구직광고
gujik gwanggo

colleague

동업자

dong-eopja

commodity exchange

상품거래소
sangpum georaeso

consolidation

합병

hapbyeong

consumer price

소비자 물가

sobija mulga

cost

원가

won-ga

cost, indirect
간접비
ganjeopbi

commercial bank

상업은행

sang-eob-eunhaeng

composite index

종합지수
jonghap jisu

consumer goods

소비재

sobijae

corporation tax

법인세

beobinse

cost analysis

원가계산

won-ga gyesan

credit bank

신용대부 은행
*sin-yong daebu
eunhaeng*

creditor	deadline
채권자	준비금 한계선
chae-gwonja	*junbigeum han-gyeseon*
deed	department store
증서	백화점
jeungseo	*baekhwajeom*
depository	discount
금고	할인
keumgo	*harin*
entrepreneur	factor
사업가	대리점
sa-eopga	*daerijeom*
fiduciary issue	fixed costs
신용발행	고정비용
sin-yong balhaeng	*gojeong biyong*
footing	foreign exchange
합계	외국환
hapgye	*oegukhwan*

goods	holder
상품	주주
sangpum	*juju*
gross profit	income tax
총 이익	소득세
chong iik	*sodeukse*
impulse buying	income, net
충동구매	순소득
chungdong gumae	*sunsodeuk*
indirect tax	index option
간접세	주가지수
ganjeopse	*juga jisu*
inflation	insolvent
통화팽창	지불불능의
tonghwa paeng chang	*jibul bulleung-ui*
insurance broker	
보험 중개인	
boheom junggaein	

PART IV
USEFUL WORDS FOR TOURING

1. Numbers and Others

You will use numbers the moment you arrive in Korea, whether it be to exchange money at the airport, pay a taxi driver, or describe the length of your stay to a customs official or hotel clerk. Followings are the frequently used cardinal and ordinal numbers, and also for specifying fractions and other useful measures.

Koreans use two kinds of numerals, one of Korean origin and the other of chinese origin. Chinese origin. Chinese numerals are generally used on money matters, the metric system, and counting floors of a building, minutes and seconds of the clock, hours, days, months and years. Here we begin with cardinal numbers.

(1) Counting Numbers

1) Cardinal Numbers

	Korean Origin		Chinese Origin	
0	영	*yeong*	영	*yeong*
1	하나	*hana*	일	*il*
2	둘	*dul*	이	*i*
3	셋	*set*	삼	*sam*

4	넷	*net*	사	*sa*
5	다섯	*daseot*	오	*o*
6	여섯	*yeoseot*	육	*yuk*
7	일곱	*ilgop*	칠	*chil*
8	여덟	*yeodeol*	팔	*pal*
9	아홉	*ahop*	구	*gu*
10	열	*yeol*	십	*sip*
11	열하나	*yeol-hana*	십일	*sibil*
12	열둘	*yeol-dul*	십이	*sibi*
13	열셋	*yeol-set*	십삼	*sipsam*
14	열넷	*yeol-net*	십사	*sipsa*
15	열다섯	*yeol-daseot*	십오	*sibo*
16	열여섯	*yeol-yeoseot*	십육	*simnyuk*
17	열일곱	*yeol-ilgop*	십칠	*sipchil*
18	열여덟	*yeol-yeodeol*	십팔	*sippal*
19	열아홉	*yeol-ahop*	십구	*sipgu*
20	스물	*seumul*	이십	*isip*
30	서른	*seoreun*	삼십	*samsip*
40	마흔	*maheun*	사십	*sasip*
50	쉰	*swin*	오십	*osip*
60	예순	*yesun*	육십	*yuksip*
70	일흔	*ilheun*	칠십	*chilsip*
80	여든	*yeodeun*	팔십	*palsip*
90	아흔	*aheun*	구십	*gusip*
99	아흔아홉	*aheun-ahop*	구십구	*gusipgu*

Up to 99 both numerals are used interchangeable. However, from 100 on, Chinese numerals are used almost exclusively.

100	(일)백	*(il)baek*
200	이백	*ibaek*
300	삼백	*sambaek*
400	사백	*sabaek*
500	오백	*obaek*
600	육백	*yukbaek*
700	칠백	*chilbaek*
800	팔백	*palbaek*
900	구백	*gubaek*
1,000	(일)천	*(il)cheon*
2,000	이천	*icheon*
3,000	삼천	*samcheon*
4,000	사천	*sacheon*
5,000	오천	*ocheon*
6,000	육천	*yukcheon*
7,000	칠천	*chilcheon*
8,000	팔천	*palcheon*
9,000	구천	*gucheon*
10,000	(일)만	*(il)man*
20,000	이만	*iman*
30,000	삼만	*samman*
40,000	사만	*saman*
50,000	오만	*oman*
60,000	육만	*yungman*
70,000	칠만	*chilman*
80,000	팔만	*palman*
90,000	구만	*guman*

100,000	(일)십만	*(il)simman*
200,000	이십만	*isimman*
300,000	삼십만	*samsimman*
400,000	사십만	*sasimman*
500,000	오십만	*osimman*
600,000	육십만	*yuksimman*
700,000	칠십만	*chilsimman*
800,000	팔십만	*palsimman*
900,000	구십만	*gusimman*
1,000,000	(일)백만	*(il)baengman*
2,000,000	이백만	*ibaengman*
3,000,000	삼백만	*sambaengman*
4,000,000	사백만	*sabaengman*
5,000,000	오백만	*obaengman*
6,000,000	육백만	*yukbaengman*
7,000,000	칠백만	*chilbaengman*
8,000,000	팔백만	*palbaengman*
9,000,000	구백만	*gubaengman*
10,000,000	(일)천만	*(il)cheonman*
20,000,000	이천만	*icheonman*
30,000,000	삼천만	*samcheonman*
100,000,000	(일)억	*(ir)eok*
1,000,000,000	십억	*sibeok*
10,000,000,000	백억	*baegeok*
100,000,000,000	천억	*cheoneok*
1,000,000,000,000	조	*jo*

e.g.	예를 들면	
	yereul deulmyeon	
307	삼백칠	
	sambaekchil	
2,549	이천오백사십구	
	icheon-obaek-sasip-gu	
33,654	삼만삼천육백오십사	
	samman-samcheon-yukbaeg-osip-sa	
1,642,350	백육십사만이천삼백오십	
	baeg-yuksipsaman-icheonsambaeg-osip	

2) Ordinal Numbers

Making cardinal numbers into ordinal numbers is a simple task in the Korean language. You simply add the suffix (beon)jjae, Note the following examples :

Korean ordinal numbers

first	첫(번)째	*cheot(beon)jjae*
second	두(번)째	*du(beon)jjae*
third	세(번)째	*se(beon)jjae*
forth	네(번)째	*ne(beon)jjae*
fifth	다섯(번)째	*daseot(beon)jjae*
sixth	여섯(번)째	*eoseot(beon)jjae*
seventh	일곱(번)째	*ilgop(beon)jjae*
eighth	여덟(번)째	*yeodeol(beon)jjae*

| ninth | 아홉(번)째 | *ahop(beon)jjae* |
| tenth | 열(번)째 | *yeol(beon)jjae* |

Chinese ordinal numbers

first	제일	*je-il*
second	제이	*je-i*
third	제삼	*je-sam*
forth	제사	*je-sa*
fifth	제오	*je-o*
sixth	제육	*je-yuk*
seventh	제칠	*je-chil*
eighth	제팔	*je-pal*
ninth	제구	*je-gu*
tenth	제십	*je-sip*

(2) Fractions and Quantities

a half _____	_____의 반	_____*ui ban*
half a _____	_____반 개	_____*ban-gae*
a quarter	사분의 일	*sabunui il*
three-quaters	사분의 삼	*sabunui sam*
a third	삼분의 일	*sambunui il*

a cup of	한 잔의	*han janui*
a dozen of	한 다스	*han daseu*
a kilogram of	일 킬로그램의	*il killogeuraemui*
a liter of	일 리터의	*il liteo-ui*
a little bit of	조금의	*jogeumui*
a lot of	많은	*maneun*
a pair of	한 쌍의	*han ssang-ui*
enough of	충분한	*chungbunhan*
too much of	너무나 많은	*neomuna maneun*
ratio	비례	*birye*
percent	백분의	*baekbunui*
twenty percent	이십 퍼센트	*isip peosenteu*
seventy percent	칠십 퍼센트	*chilsip peosenteu*
times as much	배	*bae*
six times as much	여섯 배	*yeoseot bae*
one hundred times as much	백배	*baek bae*

(3) Counting various things

| o'clock | 시 | *si* |

한 시 *han-si*　　두 시 *du-si*　　세 시 *se-si*

| hour | 시간 | sigan |

한 시간 *han-sigan* 두 시간 *du-sigan*

세 시간 *se-sigan*

| time | 번 | beon |

한 번 *han-beon* 두 번 *du-beon* 세 번 *se-beon*

| ages | 살 | sal |

한 살 *han-sal* 두 살 *du-sal* 세 살 *se-sal*

| packs | 갑 | gap |

한 갑 *han-gap* 두 갑 *du-gap* 세 갑 *se-gap*

| man | 사람 | saram |

한 사람 *han-saram* 두 사람 *du-saram*

세 사람 *se-saram*

| animals | 마리 | mari |

한 마리 *han-mari* 두 마리 *du-mari*

세 마리 *se-mari*

| bound objects such as books, notebooks, and so forth | 권 | gwon |

한 권 *han-gwon* 두 권 *du-gwon*

세 권 *se-gwon*

| houses | 채 | chae |

한 채 *han-chae* 두 채 *du-chae* 세 채 *se-chae*

| vehicles | 대 | dae |

한 대 *han-dae* 두 대 *du-dae* 세 대 *se-dae*

bottle	병	byeong

한 병 *han-byeong*　두 병 *du-byeong*

세 병 *se-byeong*

items	개	gae

한 개 *han-gae*　두 개 *du-gae*　세 개 *se-gae*

small sticks such as pencil, brush, etc	자루	jaru

한 자루 *han-jaru*　두 자루 *du-jaru*

세 자루 *se-jaru*

month	달	dal

한 달 *han-dal*　두 달 *du-dal*　세 달 *se-dal*

sheets or tickets	장	jang

한 장 *han-jang*　두 장 *du-jang*　세 장 *se-jang*

liquid(glasses or cups of.)	잔	jan

한 잔 *han-jan*　두 잔 *du-jan*　세 잔 *se-jan*

pairs of things to wear on feet of legs	켤레	kyeolle

한 켤레 *han-kyeolle*　두 켤레 *du-kyeolle*

세 켤레 *se-kyeolle*

suits(of clothes)	벌	beol

한 벌 *han-beol*　두 벌 *du-beol*　세 벌 *se-beol*

a pair, a couple	쌍	ssang

한 쌍 *han-ssang*　두 쌍 *du-ssang*

세 쌍 *se-ssang*

bowels	그릇	geureut

한 그릇 *han-geureut*　두 그릇 *du-geureut*

세 그릇 *se-geureut*

dishes	접시	*jeopsi*

한 접시 *han-jeopsi*   두 접시 *du-jeopsi*

세 접시 *se-jeopsi*

(4) Years and Counting Days

2007	이천칠년	*icheonchillyeon*
2008	이천팔년	*icheonpallyeon*

one day	하루	*haru*	일일	*iril*
two days	이틀	*iteul*	이일	*iil*
three days	사흘	*saheul*	삼일	*samil*
four days	나흘	*naheul*	사일	*sa-il*
five days	닷새	*dassae*	오일	*o-il*
six days	엿새	*yeossae*	육일	*yugil*
seven days	이레	*ire*	칠일	*chillil*
eight days	여드레	*yeodeure*	팔일	*paril*
nine days	아흐레	*aheure*	구일	*guil*
ten days	열흘	*yeolheul*	십일	*sibil*
eleven days	열하루	*yeolharu*	십일일	*sibiril*
twelve days	열이틀	*yeoriteul*	십이일	*sibiil*

(5) Counters Using Numerals

minutes	분	*bun*

일분 *il-bun*　이분 *i-bun*　삼분 *sam-bun*
사분 *sa-bun*　오분 *o-bun*

years	년	*nyeon*

일년 *il-nyeon*　이년 *i-nyeon*　삼년 *sam-nyeon*
사년 *sa-nyeon*　오년 *o-nyeon*

won (Korean money)	원	*won*

일만 원 *ilman-won*　이만 원 *iman-won*
삼만 원 *samman-won*　사만 원 *saman-won*
오만 원 *oman-won*

ages	세	*se*

일세 *il-se*　이세 *i-se*　삼세 *sam-se*
사세 *sa-se*　오세 *o-se*

floors or stories of building	층	*cheung*

일층 *il-cheung* 이층 *i-cheung* 삼층 *sam-cheung*
사층 *sa-cheung*　오층 *o-cheung*

serving portion	인분	*inbun*

일인분 *irinbun*　이인분 *iinbun*
삼인분 *saminbun*　사인분 *sa-inbun*
오인분 *o-inbun*

(6) Date

1st	일일	*iril*
2nd	이일	*iil*
3rd	삼일	*samil*
4th	사일	*sa-il*
5th	오일	*o-il*
6th	육일	*yugil*
7th	칠일	*chillil*
8th	팔일	*paril*
9th	구일	*guil*
10th	십일	*sibil*
11th	십일일	*sibiril*
12th	십이일	*sibiil*
13th	십삼일	*sipsamil*
14th	십사일	*sipsa-il*
15th	십오일	*sibo-il*
16th	십육일	*simnyugil*
17th	십칠일	*sipchiril*
18th	십팔일	*sipparil*
19th	십구일	*sipguil*
20th	이십일	*isibil*

21th	이십일일	*isibiril*
22th	이십이일	*isibiil*
23th	이십삼일	*isipsamil*
24th	이십사일	*isipsa−il*
25th	이십오일	*isibo−il*
26th	이십육일	*isimnyugil*
27th	이십칠일	*isipchiril*
28th	이십팔일	*isipparil*
29th	이십구일	*isipguil*
30th	삼십일	*samsibil*
31th	삼십일일	*samsibiril*

(7) Telling Time

A.M.	오전	*ojeon*
P.M.	오후	*ohu*
noon	정오	*jeong−o*
midnight	자정	*jajeong*
o'clock	정각	*jeonggak*

Koreans first say hours, next a list of minutes

| 1 o'clock | 한시 | *han−si* |

2 o'clock	두시	*du-si*
3 o'clock	세시	*se-si*
4 o'clock	네시	*ne-si*
5 o'clock	다섯시	*daseot-si*
6 o'clock	여섯시	*yeoseot-si*
7 o'clock	일곱시	*ilgop-si*
8 o'clock	여덟시	*yeodeol-si*
9 o'clock	아홉시	*ahop-si*
10 o'clock	열시	*yeol-si*
11 o'clock	열한시	*yeolhan-si*
12 o'clock	열두시	*yeoldu-si*
1 minute	일분	*il-bun*
2 minutes	이분	*i-bun*
3 minutes	삼분	*sam-bun*
4 minutes	사분	*sa-bun*
5 minutes	오분	*o-bun*
6 minutes	육분	*yuk-bun*
7 minutes	칠분	*chil-bun*
8 minutes	팔분	*pal-bun*
9 minutes	구분	*gu-bun*
10 minutes	십분	*sip-bun*
11 minutes	십일분	*sibil-bun*

12 minutes	십이분	*sibi-bun*
13 minutes	십삼분	*sipsam-bun*
14 minutes	십사분	*sipsa-bun*
15 minutes	십오분	*sibo-bun*
16 minutes	십육분	*simnyuk-bun*
17 minutes	십칠분	*sipchil-bun*
18 minutes	십팔분	*sippal-bun*
19 minutes	십구분	*sipgu-bun*
20 minutes	이십분	*isip-bun*
21 minutes	이십일분	*isibil-bun*
22 minutes	이십이분	*isibi-bun*
23 minutes	이십삼분	*isipsam-bun*
24 minutes	이십사분	*isipsa-bun*
25 minutes	이십오분	*isibo-bun*
26 minutes	이십육분	*isimnyuk-bun*
27 minutes	이십칠분	*isipchil-bun*
28 minutes	이십팔분	*isippal-bun*
29 minutes	이십구분	*isipgu-bun*
30 minutes	삼십분	*samsip-bun*
31 minutes	삼십일분	*samsibil-bun*
32 minutes	삼십이분	*samsibi-bun*
33 minutes	삼십삼분	*samsipsam-bun*
34 minutes	삼십사분	*samsipsa-bun*

35 minutes	삼십오분	*samsibo-bun*
36 minutes	삼십육분	*samsimnyuk-bun*
37 minutes	삼십칠분	*samsipchil-bun*
38 minutes	삼십팔분	*samsippal-bun*
39 minutes	삼십구분	*samsipgu-bun*
40 minutes	사십분	*sasip-bun*
41 minutes	사십일분	*sasibil-bun*
42 minutes	사십이분	*sasibi-bun*
43 minutes	사십삼분	*sasipsam-bun*
44 minutes	사십사분	*sasipsa-bun*
45 minutes	사십오분	*sasibo-bun*
46 minutes	사십육분	*sasimnyuk-bun*
47 minutes	사십칠분	*sasipchil-bun*
48 minutes	사십팔분	*sasippal-bun*
49 minutes	사십구분	*sasipgu-bun*
50 minutes	오십분	*osip-bun*
51 minutes	오십일분	*osibil-bun*
52 minutes	으십이분	*osibi-bun*
53 minutes	오십삼분	*osipsam-bun*
54 minutes	오십사분	*osipsa-bun*
55 minutes	오십오분	*osibo-bun*
56 minutes	오십육분	*osimnyuk-bun*
57 minutes	오십칠분	*osipchil-bun*

58 minutes	오십팔분	*osippal-bun*
59 minutes	오십구분	*osipgu-bun*
60 minutes	육십분	*yuksip-bun*
a quarter to two	두시 십오분 전	*du-si sibo-bun jeon*
a quarter after two	두시 십오분 후	*du-si sibo-bun hu*
2:15	두시 십오분	*du-si sibo-bun*
4:10	네시 십분	*ne-si sip-bun*
6:30	여섯시 삼십분	*yeoseot-si samsip-bun*

(8) Various Months

two months ago	두 달 전	*du dal jeon*
last month	지난 달	*jinan dal*
this month	이 달	*i dal*
next month	다음 달	*daeum dal*
during the month of _____	_____달 (동안에)	_____*dal (dong-ane)*
since the month of _____	_____달 이후로	_____*dal ihuro*

for the month of _______		_______달에
		_______*dale*
per month	한 달에	*han dale*
one month	한 달	*han dal*
a few months	몇 달	*myeot dal*

2. Terms For Touring

(1) Airplane / Entrance

captain	기장	*gijang*
stewardess	스튜어디스	*seutyu-eodiseu*
cabin	객실	*gaeksil*
seat number	좌석번호	*jwaseokbeonho*
boarding card	탑승권	*tapseung-gwon*
landing	착륙	*changnyuk*
take-off	이륙	*iryuk*
life jacket	구명대	*gumyeongdae*
blanket	모포	*mopo*
wet towel	물수건	*mulsugeon*
pillow	베개	*begae*
earphone	이어폰	*i-eopon*
disembark	상륙	*sangnyuk*
immigration	이민	*imin*
terminal	터미널	*teomineol*
passport	여권	*yeo-gwon*
custom	세관	*se-gwan*

baggage	수하물	*suhamul*
flight number	항공편	*hanggongpyeon*
transit	갈아타기	*garatagi*
quarantine	검역	*geom-yeok*
yellow card	예방접종증명서	*yebang jeopjong jeungmyeongseo*

(2) Signs

entrance	입구	*ipgu*
exit	출구	*chulgu*
no smoking	금연	*geumyeon*
fasten seat-belt	좌석벨트착용	*jwaseokbelteu chagyong*
transit	통과용	*tong-gwayong*
call button	초인종	*choinjong*
waiting room	대합실	*daehapsil*
danger	위험	*wiheom*
rest room	화장실	*hwajangsil*
for men	남자화장실	*namjahwajangsil*
for ladies	여자화장실	*yeojahwajangsil*
open	영업 중	*yeong-eop jung*

closed	폐점	*pyejeom*
trash	쓰레기통	*sseuregitong*
information	안내소	*annaeso*
keep out	출입금지	*churipgeumji*
mail	우편	*upyeon*

(3)Hotel

front	프론트	*peuronteu*
reservation	예약	*yeyak*
room number	객실번호	*gaeksilbeonho*
single room	1인용 방	*irinyong bang*
twin room	2인용 방	*iinyong bang*
room with bath	욕실 딸린 방	*yoksil ttallin bang*
room without bath	욕실 없는 방	*yoksil eomneun bang*
information	안내소	*annaeso*
suite	특실	*teuksil*
cloak room	짐 보관소	*jim bo-gwanso*
dining room	식당	*sikdang*
lobby	대합실	*daehapsil*
porter	짐꾼	*jimkkun*
laundry service	세탁업	*setageop*

hotel bill	계산서	*gyesanseo*
bar	바	*ba*
coffee shop	커피숍	*keopisyop*

(4) Dining

reastaurant	식당	*sikdang*
manager	지배인	*jibaein*
assistant manager	부지배인	*bujibaein*
head waiter	급사장	*geupsajang*
waiter	급사	*geupsa*
chef	주방장	*jubangjang*
bill	계산서	*gyesanseo*
menu	메뉴	*menyu*
snack bar	스낵바	*seunaekba*
cashier	계산원	*gyesanwon*
receipt	영수증	*yeongsujeung*
fork	포크	*pokeu*
knife	나이프	*na-ipeu*
spoon	스푼	*spun*
plate	접시	*jeopsi*
glass	유리컵	*yurikeop*

table	식탁	*siktak*
ashtray	재떨이	*jaetteori*
soup	수프	*supeu*
toast	토스트	*toseuteu*
butter	버터	*beoteo*
jam	잼	*jaem*
fried egg	계란프라이	*gyeranpeurai*
medium	반숙	*bansuk*
ham	햄	*haem*
vegetable soup	야채수프	*yachaesupeu*
vegetable diet	채식	*chaesik*
roast beef	로스트비프	*roseuteubipeu*
fish	생선	*saengseon*
tuna	참치	*chamchi*
bread	빵	*ppang*
sandwich	샌드위치	*saendeuwichi*
cheese	치즈	*chijeu*
beefsteak	비프스테이크	*bipeuseuteikeu*
boiled egg	삶은 계란	*salmeun-gyeran*
sausage	소시지	*sosiji*
bacon	베이컨	*beikeon*
chicken	닭고기	*dakgogi*
omelet	오믈렛	*omeullet*

salmon	연어	*yeoneo*
oyster	굴	*gul*
squid	오징어	*ojing-eo*
crab	게	*ge*
lobster	왕새우	*wangsae-u*
cabbage	양배추	*yangbaechu*
cucumber	오이	*o-i*
carrot	당근	*danggeun*
mushroom	버섯	*beoseot*
onion	양파	*yangpa*
spinach	시금치	*sigeumchi*
melon	멜론	*mellon*
watermelon	수박	*subak*
grapes	포도	*podo*
orange	오렌지	*orenji*
tangerine	귤	*gyul*
pineapple	파인애플	*pa-inaepeul*
tomato	토마토	*tomato*
potato	감자	*gamja*
eggplant	가지	*gaji*
lettuce	상추	*sangchu*
celery	샐러리	*saelleori*
apple	사과	*sagwa*

strawberry	딸기	*ttalgi*
peach	복숭아	*boksung-a*
banana	바나나	*banana*
pear	배	*bae*

(5) Drinking

beer	맥주	*maekju*
brandy	브랜디	*beuraendi*
whisky and soda	위스키소다	*wiseukisoda*
gin	진	*jin*
gin tonic	진토닉	*jintonik*
cocktail	칵테일	*kakteil*
wine	포도주	*podoju*
red wine	적포도주	*jeokpodoju*
white wine	백포도주	*baekpodoju*
champane	샴페인	*syampein*
lemonade	레몬수	*remonsu*
sugar	설탕	*seoltang*
pepper	후추	*huchu*
juice	주스	*juseu*
orange juice	오렌지주스	*orenjijuseu*

soy sauce	간장	*ganjang*
salt	소금	*sogeum*
water	물	*mul*
hot water	뜨거운 물	*tteugeoun mul*
sweet	단	*dan*
bitter	쓴	*sseun*
salty	짠	*jjan*
sour	신	*sin*
hot	매운	*mae-un*

(6) Transit

taxi	택시	*taeksi*
automobile	자동차	*jadongcha*
bus	버스	*beoseu*
rent a car	렌터카	*renteoka*
sightseeing bus	관광버스	*gwan-gwangbeoseu*
bus stop	버스정류장	*beoseujeongnyujang*
railroad	철도	*cheoldo*
train	기차	*gicha*
station	역	*yeok*
sleeping car	침대차	*chimdaecha*

dining car	식당차	*sikdangcha*
subway	지하철	*jihacheol*
steamer	기선	*giseon*
road toll	통행요금	*tonghaeng-yogeum*
gas station	주유소	*juyuso*
parking	주차	*jucha*
driver	운전기사	*unjeon-gisa*
driver's license	운전면허증	*unjeon myeonheojeung*
highway	고속도로	*gosokdoro*
interchange	인터체인지	*inteocheinji*
maximum speed	최고속도	*choegosokdo*
minimum speed	최저속도	*choejeosokdo*
ticket window	매표구	*maepyogu*
one-way ticket	편도표	*pyeondopyo*
round trip ticket	왕복표	*wangbokpyo*

(7)Sightseeing

sightseeing	관광	*gwan-gwang*
reservation	예약	*yeyak*
cancellation	취소	*chwiso*
itinerary	여정	*yeojeong*

harbor	항구	*hang-gu*
river	강	*gang*
waterfall	폭포	*pokpo*
museum	박물관	*bangmulgwan*
theater	극장	*geukjang*
embassy	대사관	*daesagwan*
library	도서관	*doseogwan*
cathedral	사원	*sawon*
garden	정원	*jeong-won*
botanical garden	식물원	*singmurwon*
cable car	케이블카	*keibeulka*
tour fare	여비	*yeobi*
map	지도	*jido*
admission fare	입장료	*ipjangnyo*
guide	안내원	*annaewon*
mountain	산	*san*
lake	호수	*hosu*
landscape	경치	*gyeongchi*
art gallery	미술관	*misulgwan*
bank	은행	*eunhaeng*
consulate	영사관	*yeongsagwan*
park	공원	*gong-won*
pagoda	탑	*tap*
zoo	동물원	*dongmurwon*

(8) Shopping

department store	백화점	*baekhwajeom*
camera shop	카메라 판매점	*kamera panmaejeom*
duty-free shop	면세점	*myeonsejeom*
glassware	유리그릇	*yurigeureut*
optician's	안경점	*an-gyeongjeom*
shoe store	양화점	*yanghwajeom*
flower shop	꽃가게	*kkotgage*
toy shop	완구점	*wan-gujeom*
stationery	문방구점	*munbanggujeom*
barber	이발소	*ibalso*
beauty shop	미장원	*mijang-won*
music store	악기점	*akgijeom*
souvenir shop	토산품점	*tosanpumjeom*
jewelry store	귀금속품점	*gwigeumsokpumjeom*
tailor shop	양복점	*yangbokjeom*
drugstore	약국	*yakguk*
bookstore	서점	*seojeom*
cosmetic shop	화장품점	*hwajangpumjeom*
chinaware	도자기	*dojagi*
gold article	금제품	*geumjepum*

silver article	은제품	*eunjepum*
cheap	싼	*ssan*
ruby	루비	*rubi*
sapphire	사파이어	*sapa-ieo*
pearl	진주	*jinju*
diamond	다이아몬드	*da-iamondeu*
jade	비취	*bichwi*
fur	모피	*mopi*
leather	가죽	*gajuk*
purse	지갑	*jigap*
necktie clasp	넥타이핀	*nekta-ipin*
wristwatch	손목시계	*sonmoksigye*
developing	필름현상	*pilleumhyeonsang*
printing	인화	*inhwa*
handbag	손가방	*son-gabang*
discount	할인	*harin*
expensive	비싼	*bissan*

(9) Illness

hospital	병원	*byeong-won*
surgeon	외과의사	*oegwauisa*

surgery	외과병원	*oegwa-byeong-won*
physician	내과의사	*naegwauisa*
dentist	치과의사	*chigwauisa*
nurse	간호원	*ganhowon*
specialist	전문의	*jeonmunui*
eye-doctor	안과의사	*an-gwauisa*
first aid	응급치료실	*eunggeupchiryosil*
bleeding	출혈	*chulhyeol*
pain	고통	*gotong*
fever	열	*yeol*
operation	수술	*susul*
fracture	골절	*goljeol*
chills	오한	*ohan*
cough	기침	*gichim*
heart disease	심장병	*simjangbyeong*
headache	두통	*dutong*
diabetes	당뇨병	*dangnyobyeong*
stomachache	복통	*boktong*
insomnia	불면증	*bulmyeonjeung*
neuralgia	신경통	*sin-gyeongtong*
eye drop	안약	*anyak*
capsule	캡슐	*kaepsyul*
cotton wool	탈지면	*taljimyeon*

prescription	처방전	*cheobangjeon*
ointment	연그	*yeongo*
tablet	알약	*allyak*
bandage	붕대	*bungdae*

(10) Names of Government Agencies

The Blue House 청와대 *cheongwadae*

Office of the Prime minister
국무총리실 *gungmuchongnisil*

Ministry of Planning and Budget
기획예산처 *gihoekyesancheo*

Ministry of Foreign Affairs and Trade
외교통상부 *oegyotongsangbu*

Ministry of Finance and Economy
재정경제부 *jaejeonggyeongjebu*

Ministry of Science & Technology
과학기술부 *gwahakgisulbu*

Ministry of Government Administration and Home
Affairs 행정자치부 *haengjeongjachibu*

Ministry of Unification 통일부 *tongilbu*

Ministry of Justice 법무부 *beopmmubu*

Government Information Agency

국정홍보처 *gukjeonghongbocheo*

Ministry of National Defense

국방부 *gukbangbu*

Ministry of Commerce, Industry and Energy

산업자원부 *saneopjawonbu*

Ministry of Agriculture & Forestry

농림부 *nongnimbu*

Ministry of Health and Welfare

보건복지부 *bogeonbokjibu*

Ministry of Information and Communication

정보통신부 *jeongbotongsinbu*

Ministry of Education & Human Resources Development

교육인적자원부 *gyoyukinjeokjawonbu*

Ministry of Culture & Tourism

문화관광부 *munhwa-gwan-gwangbu*

Ministry of Construction & Transportation

건설교통부 *geonseolgyotongbu*

Ministry of Maritime Affairs & Fisheries

해양수산부 *haeyangsusanbu*

Ministry of Environment

환경부 *hwangyeongbu*

Ministry of Labor 노동부 *nodongbu*

Ministry of Gender Equality & Family

여성가족부 *yeoseonggajokbu*

Office of Immigration

출입국관리소 *churipgukgwalliso*

The word for president is

대통령 (*daetongnyeong*)

The word for Prime Minister is

국무총리 (*gungmuchongni*)

The word for the head of each agency is

장관 (*janggwan*).

(11) Names of Various Regions and Countries

United Nations	유엔	*yu-en*
Asia	아시아	*asia*
East Asia	동아시아	*dong-asia*
Southeast Asia	동남아시아	*dongnamasia*
South Asia	남아시아	*namasia*
Europe	유럽	*yureop*
Middle East	중동	*jungdong*
North America	북미	*bungmi*
South America	남미	*nammi*
Central America	중남미	*jungnammi*

Australia	호주	*hoju*
New Zealand	뉴질랜드	*nyujillaendeu*
Philippines	필리핀	*pillipin*
Indonesia	인도네시아	*indonesia*
Malaysia	말레이시아	*malleisia*
Singapore	싱가포르	*singgaporeu*
Thailand	태국	*taeguk*
Taiwan	대만	*daeman*
China	중국	*jungguk*
Hong Kong	홍콩	*hongkong*
Japan	일본	*ilbon*
U.S.A	미국	*miguk*
Canada	캐나다	*kaenada*
U.K.	영국	*yeongguk*
India	인도	*indo*
Russia	러시아	*reosia*
Pacific region	태평양지역	*taepyeongyang jiyeog*

Korean Conversation

발 행   2016년 03월 15일

저 자   신명섭, 조홍섭
발행인   이재명
발행처   삼지사

등록번호 제406-2011-000021호
주 소   경기도 파주시 산남로 47-10
Tel   031)948-4502, 948-4564   Fax 031)948-4508
홈페이지 www.samjisa.com